an ARCHITECTURE

An ARCHITECTURE Notebook builds on the foundation of Simon Unwin's previous book *Analysing ARCHITECTURE* (Routledge, 1997). Using numerous examples, illustrated with clear line drawings, this volume describes and illustrates the many powers attaching to one of the most basic architectural elements – the wall.

Exploring its primitive origins in relation to the natural walls of cliffs and caves, illustrating the effects and opportunities of its evolution into the artificial and then the naked cave, and examining the ways in which it is used to frame and organise the spaces of our lives, this book presents the wall as one of the most powerful inventions of the mind.

Like its predecessor, *An ARCHITECTURE Notebook* is a stimulus to thinking about what one can do with architecture. It offers an example to student architects of how they might keep their own architecture notebooks, collecting ideas, sorting strategies, generally expanding their understanding of the potential of architecture to change the world.

Simon Unwin is a Senior Lecturer at The Welsh School of Architecture, Cardiff University. He has lived in Britain and Australia, and also taught architecture in Israel, Sweden, and the United States.

Some reviews of Simon Unwin's previous book, *Analysing Architecture*:

"Unwin chooses to look at the underlying elements of architecture rather than, as is more usual, at the famous names, styles, movements and chronology of the genre. This rejection of the conventional art-historical approach can lead to interesting conclusions... it is all presented cogently and convincingly through the medium of Unwin's own drawings."

Hugh Pearman, <u>The Sunday Times</u>

"One would have no hesitation in recommending this book to new students: it introduces many ideas and references central to the study of architecture. The case studies are particularly informative. A student would find this a useful aid to identifying the many important issues seriously engaged with in Architecture."

Lorraine Farrelly, <u>Architectural Design</u>

"The text has been carefully written to avoid the use of jargon and it introduces architectural ideas in a straightforward fashion. This, I suspect, will give it a well-deserved market beyond that of architects and architectural students."

Barry Russell, <u>Environments BY DESIGN</u>

"From the campsites of primitive man to the sophisticated structures of the late twentieth century, architecture as an essential function of human activity is explained clearly, and illustrated with the author's own excellent drawings. Highly recommended as a well-organized and readable introduction."

medals@win-95.com, <u>Amazon.com website</u>

"This book establishes a systematic method in analyzing architecture. It explains how architectural elements are combined together to form designs that could relate an appropriate sense of 'place' specific to the programme as well as the environment surrounding it. The book is well illustrated with diagrams and examples. An extremely useful introductory guide for those who want to learn more about the basics of architecture."

nikana99@hotmail.com, <u>Amazon.com website</u>

"The most lucid and readable introduction to architecture I have read."

Professor Roger Stonehouse, Manchester School of Architecture

an **ARCHITECTURE** notebook

Simon Unwin

London and New York

First published 2000
by Routledge
11 New Fetter Lane, London EC4P 4EE

Simultaneously published in the USA and Canada
by Routledge
29 West 35th Street, New York, NY 10001

Printed and bound in Great Britain by
St. Edmundsbury Press, Bury St. Edmunds, Suffolk.

Publisher's Note.
This book has been prepared using camera-ready copy supplied by
the author.

British Library Cataloguing in Publication Data
A catalogue record for this book is available from the British Library.

Library of Congress Cataloging in Publication Data
A catalog record for this book has been requested.

ISBN 0-415-22873-5 (hbk)
ISBN 0-415-22874-3 (pbk)

"Modern builders need a classification of architectural factors irrespective of time and country, a classification by essential variation.... In architecture more than anywhere we are the slaves of names and categories, and so long as the whole field of past architectural experiment is presented to us accidentally only under historical schedules, designing architecture is likely to be conceived as scholarship rather than as the adaptation of its accumulated powers to immediate needs...."

W.R. Lethaby – *Architecture*, 1912, pp.8-9.

for students of architecture

CONTENTS

PREFACE

PREFACE

Defending armies have their backs to it; athletes hit it; the weakest go to it; teachers find themselves talking to it... or putting another brick in it; ancient kings see the writing on it; deserters are stood in front of it, and shot; children hide behind it... parents bash their heads against it; drunks walk into it; nursery rhyme characters sit on it... and then fall off it, or fly away; the dead are laid by it; the desperate urinate against it; disturbed neighbours knock on it; the self-deluded paper over the cracks in it; equivocators position themselves on it; businesses are driven to it; religious people worship at it; the distressed turn their faces to it; the mad go up it; absconders go over it; the frustrated are driven up it; you can encounter one of silence, sound, heat, hostility...; or ride one of death.

Plurally, they have ears, and tongues; or may be 'Chinese'; secrets are kept between 'these' four of them; eavesdroppers put their ears to them; spies drill holes in them; lovers, or vandals, scratch their initials into their surfaces; insomniacs count sheep jumping over them; those with whom no-one will dance stand by them, as '—flowers'; the wicked are put behind them; witches were immured within them. Biblically, Jericho's were demolished by the sound of Joshua's trumpets.

Why do we use the wall so often as a negative metaphor? Why dumb, frustrating, obstructive, deceitful, divisive? How would we live without walls? We make them everywhere, and yet it seems we also hate them.

Are walls necessarily bad? Are walls 'veils of shame', antidotes to the 'fall from grace' by which we organise our world and make it bearably habitable: socially, practically, environmentally, psychologically, spiritually...? Without them would we live in a morally better, 'natural', state? Or are walls instruments of good, fundamental to civilisation..., one of the means by which we take control of the world and make it how we want it to be?

Walls are products of our minds, and incarcerate us. They soak up our lives, and give back blankness. They make for us extra 'skulls' in which to hide, and cells to shut things away. We depend on them, and yet resent our dependency. We see them as barriers to freedom and communality, but at the same time realise that those same barriers help us keep peace and sanity. Walls may aggravate our claustrophobic instincts, but they also comfort our innate agoraphobia. They have two sides to them, literally and metaphorically.

The wall is sometimes seen as the

blank canvas of architecture, a surface onto which 'architecture' is applied. But it is much more than that. The wall itself is one of the most powerful instruments available to an architect. By the arrangement of walls the architect sets out the spatial matrices within which our lives are lived.

Walls are ubiquitous; so much so that they are taken for granted, seen but unnoticed. And their effects are so strong that they may be sublimated, left beneath conscious acknowledgement. Perhaps walls are more powerful than we like to think.

When Philip Larkin wrote 'Church Going' (1955, right) he didn't mention the church's walls. In the poem he knows they are there but ignores them, not seeing them but sensible to their effects. The door he steps through would not be necessary but for the walls; the sense of entering, of moving from a bright outside to a dim inside, would be impossible. The separation from the ordinary everyday world that suffuses the poem's description of the internal atmosphere of the church depends on the unacknowledged walls. They define and channel a route through the church's space; from graveyard, through entrance, along nave, to the "holy end". They provide the backdrop for the brownish "sprawlings of flowers" and the "brass and stuff" on the altar. They help give the church its "tense, musty, unignorable silence". The walls support the apparently "almost new" roof. They echo the poet's louder than intended "'Here endeth'". They do not need to be mentioned because they are necessarily there. The sacred cell they make is fundamental, and assumed.

Architects are resented, perhaps because they put up walls. Like doctors giving medicine, judges sentences, teachers lessons, sergeants drill, politicians laws, game-makers rules..., the imposition of discipline, though recognised reluctantly as beneficial, is disliked. Walls are an assertion of control, of order, a manifestation of civilisation... of the world ordered by the mind. They liberate by restriction; give peace by shutting out noise; shelter by closing out the weather; privacy by screening from the public; security by sealing off space from malicious strangers. Like freedom, they constitute a negative that has positive effects. The city, the product and home of civilisation, would be inconceivable without its walls.

The freedom walls give is a freedom from exposure. They allow proximity with separation. They allow hot places to be

"Once I am sure there's nothing going on
I step inside, letting the door thud shut.
Another church: matting, seats, and stone,
And little books; sprawlings of flowers, cut
For Sunday, brownish now; some brass and stuff
Up at the holy end; the small neat organ;
And a tense, musty, unignorable silence,
Brewed God knows how long. Hatless, I take off
My cycle-clips in awkward reverence,

"Move forward, run my hand around the font.
From where I stand, the roof looks almost new –
Cleaned or restored? Someone would know: I don't.
Mounting the lectern, I peruse a few
Hectoring large-scale verses, and pronounce
'Here endeth' much more loudly than I meant.
The echoes snigger briefly. Back at the door
I sign the book, donate an Irish sixpence,
Reflect the place was not worth stopping for."

from Philip Larkin – 'Church Going' (1955).

Reference for 'conceptual organisation, intellectual structuring, identification of place':
Simon Unwin – *Analysing Architecture*, pp.12-17.

within a few inches of cool, dry humid, light dark, private public, quiet noisy, old new, sacred profane, beautiful ugly, lonely congregational, radioactive radioinactive, dangerous safe, wealthy poor, dirty clean, focused dissipated, dynamic static, small extensive, ordered amorphous, there here, your my.... Walls can be used to contrive opposites, and allow them to be close neighbours. But our discomfort with their closure of space is evident in the pictures, the illusions of three-dimensional space, we put on their blank, forbidding surfaces.

This book is not about the technology of building walls, it is about the roles walls play in architecture considered as *conceptual organisation, intellectual structuring, identification of place*. It is about walls as instruments of the minds of those who dispose and arrange them. It is about what walls can be used to do: how they interplay with the ways space, on the surface of the earth and under the sky, is occupied; how they contribute to and affect lived experience; how they help in orientation and the management of the world around.

Walls are agents and symbolic manifestations of the order, and the conflicts, of life in the world. In Nazareth, in 1999, the Muslim community decided to build a mosque alongside the Christian Basilica of the Annunciation. It seems to have been a political as well as a religious gesture, which upset the Christian community in the town and provoked unrest. Before work properly started on the building the Muslims took possession of the place, occupying it as if the mosque was already there. They marked out a square with curbstones, oriented to Mecca. Inside were carpets, outside was the tarmac of the car park site, with neat lines of shoes. The Muslims used this square of carpets as the mosque. On hot days it was shaded with cloth. Worshippers washed their feet and hands in nearby water troughs. The *mihrab*, the symbolic doorway to Mecca, was marked with a white plastic garden chair. Steps formed the *minbar*, the 'pulpit'. And the *minaret* from which the *muezzin* called the faithful to prayer was a scaffolding pole with loudspeakers attached. With all this in place the mosque already existed, but without a building. The essential elements of its architecture were there..., complete with the illusion of 'walls' psychologically as strong as any built barriers, but through which the statement of worship, and symbolic possession of place, could be displayed to the world.

ACKNOWLEDGEMENTS

Adam Sharr, Adèle Mills,
Alan Lipman, Alan Paddison,
Alwyn Jones, Andy Carr,
Anna Radcliffe, Baruch Baruch,
Bob Croydon, Bob Fowles,
Bob MacLeod, Bob Tranter,
Caroline Mallinder, Charlie MacCallum,
Chris Powell, Christine Hawley,
Colin Hockley, David Gray,
David Grech, David McLees,
David Shalev, David Unwin,
Dean Hawkes, Dewi Prys Thomas,
Dick Powell, Doug Frayn,
Douglas Hogg, Duncan Fraser,
Eurwyn Wiliam, Flora Samuel,
Frans Nicholas, Geoff Cheason,
Gerallt Nash, Gill Unwin,
Hanan Laskin, Howard Lawrence,
Irit Tsaraf-Netanyahu, Ivor Richards,
James Armitage, James Unwin,
Jane MacDonald, Jeremy Dain,
Jeremy Lowe, Jo Odgers, John Carter,
John Eynon, John Punter,
Jonathan Vining, Judi Loach,

Kieren Morgan, Leon Conway,
Lindsay Evans, Liora Bar Am Shahal,
Lydia Mallison-Jones, Malcolm Parry,
Mary Comerford, Mary Unwin,
Matthew Williams, Michael Brawne,
Michael Chaito, Mike Harries,
Neil Leach, Nick Bullock, Nigel Marsh,
Olle Wahlström, Patrick Hannay,
Patrick Hodgkinson, Paul Bulkeley,
Peter Harrison, Pierre d'Avoine,
Prys Morgan, Rebecca Casey,
Richard Dean, Richard Haslam,
Richard Parnaby, Richard Silverman,
Richard Weston, Robert Wall,
Robert Wallbridge, Robin Campbell,
Roger Stonehouse, Rose Clements,
Sally Daniels, Sara Furse,
Simon Michaels, Sophia Psarra,
Stanley Cox, Steve Izenour,
Sue and Pete Ryrie, Sunand Prasad,
Sylvia Harris, Tim Barton, Tim Unwin,
Tom Lloyd, Tony Aldrich, Tony Neales,
Wayne Forster...
                              ... and lots of others.

"An infinitely more valuable insight into the significance of the chorus was furnished by Schiller in the famous Preface to his Bride of Messina, *where the chorus is seen as a living wall which tragedy draws about itself in order to achieve insulation from the actual world, to preserve its ideal ground and its poetic freedom."*

Friedrich Nietzsche, translated by Francis Golffing – *The Birth of Tragedy* (1871), 1956.

For your many and various, often unwitting but always valuable, contributions to the making of this book, over many years... thanks.

INTRODUCTION

INTRODUCTION

"The intellect is a cleaver; it discerns and rifts its way into the secret of things. I do not wish to be any more busy with my hands than is necessary. My head is hands and feet. I feel all my best faculties concentrated in it. My instinct tells me that my head is an organ for burrowing, as some creatures use their snout and forepaws, and with it I would mine and burrow my way through these hills. I think that the richest vein is somewhere hereabouts; so by the divining rod and thin rising vapours I judge; and here I will begin to mine."

Henry David Thoreau – *Walden*, 1854.

"The healthy mind discovers itself, not by looking within, but by examining the outer world, comparing its experiences, and inquiring into their mutual relations."

Roger Hinks – *The Gymnasium of the Mind*, 1984.

Reference for Le Corbusier on the Athenian Acropolis and in Pompeii:
Le Corbusier, edited, annotated, and translated by Ivan Zaknic in collaboration with Nicole Pertuiset – *Journey to the East*, 1987.

Reference for Louis Kahn's sketches:
Eugene J. Johnson – *Drawn from the Source: the travel sketches of Louis I. Kahn*, 1996.

Reference for Alvar Aalto's sketches:
Göran Schildt – *Sketches: Alvar Aalto*, 1978.

A notebook is an annexe to the brain – a storeroom and a study. Used to keep information that might be forgotten or lost, a notebook is also a place for *making sense* – a refuge where a mind can play with ideas, exploring their ramifications, and reflecting on their relationships.

My notebooks contain a mess of information and ideas collected while trying to make sense of architecture. They are chaotic: full of sketched plans and sections, scribbled extracts from texts, and repetitions of observations which each time they were written down must have seemed like fresh insights.

This published *Architecture Notebook* has to be more disciplined, with the clutter rearranged into some sort of order... given its own 'architecture'.

Many architects have used ideas that they have found in the work of others and the world around them. Even those acknowledged as the most inventive and original can be seen, from their sketchbooks, to have collected ideas from their explorations. The sketchbooks of Le Corbusier, Louis Kahn, Alvar Aalto, and many others, illustrate their acquisitiveness, their receptivity to ideas they might be able to develop in their own work.

When Alvar Aalto visited the ancient Greek site at Delphi he drew the place of performance, and later, in his own work in Finland (for example, at the university at Ottaniemi and in the design for his own studio), used what he learnt about relationships between spectators, focus, and topography.

When Louis Kahn drew expressively the brick bastions of the cathedral at Albi, or the sun-drenched walls of an Arabic city, he inculcated his own capacity for architecture with their charged energy, and the density of solid, structured mass in bright sunlight.

When Le Corbusier spent time on the Acropolis in Athens he carefully drew the plans and the sections of the Propylaea and of the Erectheum. By doing this he translated the direct experience they presented to his senses into the abstract conventions of architectural drawing, and thereby assimilated in his own mind the intellectual structure given them by their original architects in response to brief and conditions. When he visited Pompeii he reconstructed in his sketchbook the columned front of the Temple of Jupiter, evoking in his mind and providing for his eyes the rhythm of the screened view it would have given of the Forum in front of it. He revelled in what this activity of thought-fully drawing what he saw gave him. His engagement with the buildings he experienced made him more aware of, and able to exploit in his own work, the possibilities of architecture. It involved him with the minds of others who have tackled the problems and adventure of architecture. It enlarged and refined his range and aspiration as an architect.

The premises on which this *Architecture Notebook* builds were laid out in *Analysing Architecture* (Routledge, 1997). There are five.

First: architecture is considered as an intellectual activity, which consists in giving intellectual structure. Architecture draws on the faculty of the mind to put things in some sort of order, to give them form. Viollet-le-Duc wrote that "art is... the form given to a thought", but for the artist (architect) it is, in the first instance, the other way around: art (architecture) is the thought given to (which determines) form. Art (architecture) is intellectual activity, before it is product.

Second: although all the mind's formations can be said, metaphorically, to have their 'architecture' – plays, novels, poems, symphonies, statutes, paintings,

expeditions... – the rudimentary concern of architects is to give intellectual structure to the organisation of (a portion of) the physical world, in the identification of place(s).

Third: architecture as identification of place may involve nothing more than choice – the choice of a grassy bank as a seat, for example – but architecture also drives the alteration of the world through building (which includes excavation and demolition). 'Building' is the primary *means* by which architecture is given physical manifestation.

Fourth: though not primarily a language, architecture may be compared with language. Both seem to depend on primal instincts: language on the desire (need) to generate formal and consistent codes for communication; architecture on the desire (need) to organise the physical world into places. Both are media through which constructs are applied to (imposed on) the world. Where the primary burden of language is *meaning*, the primary burden of architecture is *place*. Both language and architecture are intellectual activities involving the mind in making sense of the world around. Neither can be described accurately as a process of finding a solution by analysing a problem. In both there

Reference for "Art is... the form given to a thought":

Eugene Viollet-le-Duc, translated by Benjamin Bucknall – *Lectures on Architecture* (1860), 1877, p.24.

"The search is what everyone would undertake if he were not stuck in the everydayness of his own life. To be aware of the possibility of the search is to be onto something. Not to be onto something is to be in despair."

Walker Percy – *The Moviegoer*, quoted in Lawrence Weschler – *Seeing is Forgetting the Name of the Thing One Sees: a life of contemporary artist Robert Irwin*, 1982, p.1.

are patterns, strategies, structures available in common, which can be applied to situations, and which facilitate while not determining content. Skill, both in language and in architecture, seems to require changes in the brain which can only be acquired through practice. Both involve drawing upon reserves built up in the memory, and discrimination in their application....

And fifth: if architecture may be compared to language, then learning *to do* architecture might be comparable to learning language. That is, acquisition is assisted by thoughtful conscious exposure to how it is (has been) done by others. One learns something about how to use language by listening to those who speak it, reading those who write it, and by trying to make sense of their intentions and the means they use to achieve them. One may learn something about how to do architecture by examining the work of those who do it, and by trying to make sense of their intentions and the means they use to achieve them.

In language there is a long-established and accepted conceptual framework for grammatical analysis. *Analysing Architecture* tentatively offered the beginnings of such a conceptual framework for the analysis of architecture. *An Architecture Notebook* continues this task, looking at

one of the elements of architecture in detail.

The subject of this *Notebook* is the wall. It looks more intently and in detail at the roles played by just one of the 'basic elements' of architecture identified in *Analysing Architecture*. It considers the many ways the wall is used by the designing mind in imposing its intellectual structures on the world.

Taking this brief – to make sense of the wall as an instrument of architecture – this *Notebook* presents an exploration of examples, from many times and places, of the ways walls are used and the different things they can do. The aim is to inform the adventure of architectural design with an awareness of possibilities, to identify some of the powers walls offer architects.

The result is a series of thematic chapters discussing the various ways in which walls are used in architecture:

Chapter One – 'Wall' – makes some basic observations on the ubiquity of walls and what they do. It considers how walls influence and affect our experience of the world. It also looks at some of the consequences of the ways architects arrange the layout of walls through the abstraction of conventional architectural drawing.

21

Chapter Two – 'Wall as Surface' – begins by looking at walls found in nature – cliffs and caves – and considers our primitive and psychological relationship with walls as surfaces between space we can occupy and solid that we cannot.

Chapter Three – 'Primitive Built Walls' – speculates on the invention of some basic types of wall (for example, the retaining wall, the partition wall, and the enclosing wall) and notes some of the things they enable architects to do.

Chapter Four – 'Artificial Cave' – examines the roles played by walls in making artificial caves, and notes the emergence of related spatial geometries.

Chapter Five – 'Naked Cave' – considers the consequences of the emergence of the artificial cave from its subterranean state, exposing the outside surfaces of walls as screens for display, and allowing the manipulation of natural light in internal spaces.

Chapter Six – 'Expression' – looks at the many and various ways in which walls can be expressive: of location, tradition, culture, identity, status, imagination, aspiration, knowledge, sophistication, skill,

resources... even philosophy, and a sense of humour.

Chapter Seven – 'Enclosure' – presents examples illustrating the different things walled enclosures have been used to do: concealment, protection, containment, orientation....

Chapter Eight – 'Labyrinth and Datum' – looks at ways walls are used to prevent and channel movement, and to manipulate serial experience, as well as the ways they can enhance legibility by providing datums to help people keep track of where they are.

Chapter Nine – 'Inhabited Wall' – looks at ways architects exploit the zone within walls, between 'inside' and 'outside'. It considers ways in which architects have tried to obscure the presence of walls, and ways they have created inhabited walls.

Chapter Ten – 'Sound, Heat, Light' – looks at ways walls are used in relation to some of the 'modifying elements of architecture'.

A 'Postscript' is followed by a 'Select Bibliography' of texts that amplify the themes discussed in the chapters.

WALL

WALL

"The elements of the house can be derived only from nature: the primary datum of the wall-separated space is the unlimited mass of the earth with the limitless space above it; so the limited mass of the walls must also be drawn from the earth in order to withdraw a limited piece of space from the space of nature."

Dom H. van der Laan, translated by Richard Padovan – *Architectonic Space: fifteen lessons on the disposition of the human habitat*, 1983.

Along with the 'defined area of ground' (dancing floor, yard, football pitch...) and the 'marker' (gravestone, church steeple, lighthouse), the 'wall' is one of the most basic elements of architecture. Walls frame our existence. The things we do relate in some way to walls more often than not. Walls mark out the territories of our lives; they provide us with shelter and privacy; they support the roofs over our heads; they protect our belongings, and keep out strangers; we project images onto them; play games against them... and use them for many other things besides. We build them, and when they are built they set the space in which our actions and relationships take place. We can change them, and the spatial order they determine, but not without effort. Walls become old, and part of our established environment... as if they have been there for ever... as if they are part of nature.

The origins of wall building are lost in the immemorial past. Even the oldest surviving fragments must have been preceded by generations of walls built from less durable materials and construction, which have not survived even as archaeological traces. But, although it may seem as if there have always been walls, the built wall was once an invention, a new idea.

As architects we build walls, or cause them to be built, in particular positions for particular purposes. The built wall is an instrument of the mind, and a powerful one. A wall manifests its architect's purposes (or an architect's interpretation of a client's or user's purposes). It is born of intention and infused with attitude.

Intentions behind wall building vary and can have different interpretations. They may be to protect or acquire, to include or exclude, to bring together or divide, to clarify or confuse, to provide support or impose a burden, to shade or reflect light, to make a silent place or enhance sound, to keep cool or warm....

Attitudes might be altruistic or selfish, hubristic or stoical, established or subversive, opportunistic or reactive, assertive or submissive....

Walls can have many kinds of significance: moral, social, personal, political, military, philosophical, symbolic, religious, psychological, aesthetic, poetic....

Walls deny space. A wall is an intentional obstruction to free and uninterrupted movement. In denying space walls also 'create space', or at least mould space into defined forms. In 'creating' or defining space, they contribute to the making of *places*.

Walls exclude. They are built to keep things out: enemies, weather, thieves, animals, light, radiation, sound, cold, wind, heat, rain....

Walls contain. They are built to keep things in: cold, heat, children, livestock, belongings, water, earth....

Walls protect. They are built to keep things safe.

Walls screen. They are built to hide things from view.

Walls support. They are built to hold up roofs and floors.

Walls have surfaces. We draw, paint, carve, stick, hang, project... images on them.

Walls divide. They have two sides – physically, and metaphorically. They compress and make tangible distances between things by making a solid barrier that provides security and separation. They extend the territory of what they contain to a precise boundary, and set limits to what is inside and what is outside. With walls space can be used more economically than without. The compact city is made possible by walls.

Walls are built by the application of physical effort to available material. The materials from which walls can be built range from stone to straw, from timber to titanium, from mud, to brick, to concrete, to glass... one can even build walls of paper or cardboard.

The structural strength and stability of walls can be calculated. One can worry about how a wall can be made weatherproof, or soundproof. One can calculate how well a wall will insulate a warm interior from a cold exterior, or a cool interior from a hot exterior; and predict whether certain conditions will produce problems of condensation on its surfaces or within its fabric.

But the primary concerns when proposing a wall are to do with the organisation of space: where exactly should it be; why should it be just 'there'; what dimensions should it have; why should it be just that length, height, thickness...; and, what will it do; will it do what is wanted; will it do something that is not wanted? The fabric of buildings interrelates with the life they accommodate, which takes place in space and time. The relationships between solid and space, between walls and life, are vital.

Once you think about the walls around you, and what they are doing, you start to understand some of the ways they condition

26

"Space is a doubt: I have constantly to mark it, to designate it. It's never mine, never given to me, I have to conquer it."

Georges Perec, translated by John Sturrock – *Species of Spaces*, 1974.

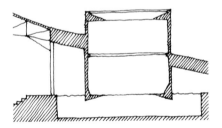

James Turrell has produced a number of works which use walls to transform one's perception of the sky into a moving abstract picture. In Heavy Water *(Poitiers, 1991) a cube of space, defined by its four walls, is suspended over water. You enter the space by swimming under the walls, and then sit on the ledge, at exactly the water's surface, to watch the sky through the open roof, its reflection on the water, and the sunlight and shadows on the walls.*

lives, affect experience, make some things possible, and deny others.

Walls in memory and imagination....

Imagine land open to the horizon: a beach, a desert, a rolling plain, vast fields of stubble.... There is a small enclosure of walls taller than the level of your eyes. Step, or perhaps you have to climb, inside. Think of the difference being inside from being outside: the shelter from the wind; the sound is different; the sun and shadows; the relaxing privacy; the definition of the finite space; the surfaces; the corners; the sense of security; you lean on the wall or sit on the floor and look at the sky....

Remember entering a walled garden. Approaching the gate from outside you see a blank wall, in shadow, framing a view into sunlit colour. Passing through, you are in a different world, a different climate, a 'paradise' made possible by the wall.

Entering a gateway in the wall of an old city – Dubrovnik, Nicosia, Jerusalem, York – is like penetrating the skin of an organism; the vitality inside, channelled in alleyways, is in stark contrast to the blank, impervious face of the walls from outside, which from within the city are almost invisible, masked by the accretions of the city's life.

Sometimes you find yourself walking alongside a wall, or even between two walls, with them steering your path, directing your line of sight, focusing on your goal, or perhaps gradually revealing where you are going.

Sometimes you have the opportunity to walk on top of a wall, with that sense of transcendence, of treading a path suspended between two worlds: your garden one side, a neighbour's the other; the city one side, the sea or the unformed world the other; a small step one side, a giant leap the other; the protected ward of a castle one side, the world of enemies the other...; the top of the wall straight or snaking ahead of you, defining your only route; the strange viewpoints and alignments, looking over, across, down, along...; somehow separate from ordinary life, in a special zone, on a special plane, above.

You go to the cinema. Your time is spent staring at a wall..., or at least, images projected on a wall; and the essential darkness, comfort, and separation from the ordinary everyday world is provided by walls.

You go to an art gallery. The pictures depend on the walls, which also affect the quality of light and the acoustic. Your path through the exhibition is guided by those walls too. Waiting for a friend, you sit on a wall outside.

You go to a gym, or sports centre. Maybe you hit a ball against a wall...; maybe there is a place where you can climb a wall, to practise for real rock faces; some of the equipment relies on a wall; the list of activities is displayed on a wall....

The examples go on and on.... There is an extremely high likelihood that, while reading this book, you are in some sort of relationship with a wall, or set of walls that establish the place where you are. The walls of my study, here now as I write, provide me with the quiet and privacy to concentrate; they carry the floor and roof above; they contain warmth and reflect light; their (orthogonal) arrangement conditions the layout of furniture – desk, drawing table, piano...; they support numerous bookshelves; and are covered with pictures, maps, notes.... They frame me working, writing, drawing.

Walls in architects' drawings....

The drawn plan of a work of architecture can be its most telling representation. A horizontal slice, looking down, perpendicularly towards the surface of the earth, a plan shows an organisation of space. Most basic architectural elements –

defined area of ground, platform, pit, wall, column, door, window, marker... even roof – can be indicated on a plan... as an abstraction.

Architectural plans can be beautiful things. Sometimes their beauty is graphic, immediate, like that of an abstract painting or drawing. But a more profound beauty can lie in the thought they contain. Like music written on a stave, they have to be 'read', in terms both of the reality they propose and the ideas that underlie them.

They don't work in words, yet the plans architects draw when doing architecture are philosophical. Their philosophy can be banal, but in some cases it may be sublime, penetrating, displaying a profound understanding of what it is to be in the world. In composing a plan an intellect makes sense of a part of the surface of the earth, organising it according to understanding and imagination, responding and relating to its conditions, and introducing (overlaying, interleaving, intertwining...) ideas. A sublime plan may be simple, or intricate; it may be intelligent, subtle, inspired, poetic, mystical....

The medium in which a plan's philosophy is ultimately intended to operate is that combination of space-time-matter

"The dark stone wall looked back at me with composure, shut off in a deep twilight, sunk in a dream of its own. And there was no gateway anywhere and no pointed arch; only the dark unbroken masonry. With a smile I went on, giving it a friendly nod. 'Sleep well. I will not wake you. The time will come when you will be pulled down or plastered with covetous advertisements. But for the present, there you stand, beautiful and quiet as ever, and I love you for it.'"

Hermann Hesse, translated by Basil Creighton
– *Steppenwolf* (1927), 1980, p.48.

which accommodates life in the physical world. The plan in drawing is an expedient abstraction, allowing an intellect to explore and manoeuvre, in a lubricated way, propositions for manipulating space-time-matter(-life) without premature and expensive consequence – i.e. without having to build – in the real world.

The surface (paper or computer screen) on which a plan is drawn is a meta-phorical world surface, occupied and changed in the imagination of the designing mind. When it is drawing-planning-designing, the mind enters this world intently and exclusively, and, through 'dialogue' with the successive drafts it produces, comes to a conclusion about what might be. The process is a dialectic, inductive and deductive, questioning soliloquy in many dimensions, played out through

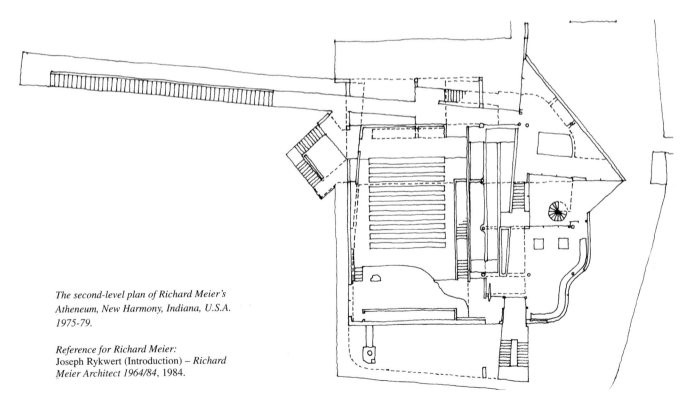

The second-level plan of Richard Meier's Atheneum, New Harmony, Indiana, U.S.A. 1975-79.

Reference for Richard Meier:
Joseph Rykwert (Introduction) – *Richard Meier Architect 1964/84*, 1984.

the medium of two-dimensional drawing – a primal and compelling intellectual adventure.

A line on a plan is very often the representation of a wall's surface in reality. Although it shows a *horizontal* slice through a work of architecture, one of the primary purposes in drawing a plan is to determine the positions of *vertical* surfaces – walls that demarcate, delimit, control, govern, modify, manage, organise space and the horizontal occupation of it on the ground. Drawn plans tend, pre-eminently, to be 'about' walls. Lines on a drawn plan *are* walls and, when they have been built, the walls themselves are 'lines' 'drawn' in the real world to establish a matrix of spatial separations and relationships.

A drawn plan, and the work of architecture realised from it, is a visible externalisation of the cogitations of a designing intellect. Its 'language' consists of the elements of architecture. Its burden is the organisation of space... and more.

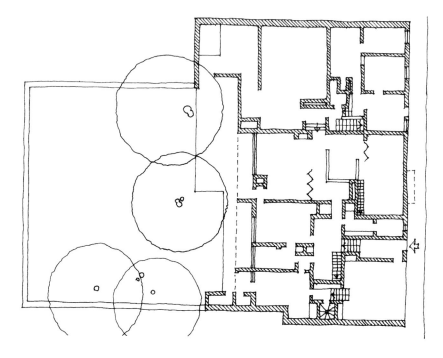

This is the ground-floor plan of Luis Barragán's house in Mexico City (1947). The house is a subtle composition of walls which organise its space, reflect light, conceal and reveal, protect....

Reference for Barragán's house:
Raúl Rispa (editor) – *Barragán, the complete works*, 1996, pp.112-23.

"The process by which a city is divided begins with a man painting a line on the ground. This first step is being made under British Army supervision. The line starts at the sidewalk on the west side of Potsdamerstrasse."

Caption to a photograph of early preparations for dividing the city of Berlin in the aftermath of the Second World War, in:
A. Balfour – *Berlin: the politics of order, 1737-1989*, 1990, p.186.

Drawing a plan, to scale on paper, allows the intellect to grasp, generate, and assess the effects of organisational ideas more subtle and more sophisticated than would be possible through the act of building in reality. But the mind drawing in abstract can also miss (be ignorant of) subtleties and problems that might arise in the realised product. A drawing can allow the intellect to indulge itself with what might be (in some way) 'inappropriate' ideas – ideas that may seem to work 'on paper' but don't when realised. Walls in reality can be manifestations of these dreams on paper.

The efficacy of the abstraction depends on the intelligence of the intellect. That is, the eventual 'success' of the plan in physical realisation depends on how 'appropriate' the introduced ideas may be, and how thoroughly the intellect understands what it is drawing in abstract, and what will result in reality. Of course issues of 'appropriateness', 'success', and of whether a plan does or does not 'work' in reality, can be contentious. Walls can be aggressive, intellectually as well as militarily.

Drawn plans, like written philosophy, can clarify, but, being abstractions, they can also oversimplify, omit, obscure, or deceive. Nevertheless, drawing plans is one of the principal ways in which an architect's intellect philosophises about how the world may and should be arranged.

Like language, plans have their conventions. Also, the means and instruments and techniques of drawing may condition the philosophising.

The underlying assumptions that make plans a useful abstract way of developing and representing works of architecture relate to the nature of walls.

Whether they are real or implied, when one is looking at a plan, one is looking at walls and the ways they organise space. A plan is a diagram of the mind's organisation of space (into places), and organising space (usually) involves walls of some kind – masonry walls, fences, hedges, moats, ditches, dykes... even imaginary implied walls (like those of the temporary mosque in Nazareth described on page 15).

The plan is an abstract description of the intellectual structure of a work. It has been associated through history with a conception of architecture primarily as a matter of wall building (which itself relates to the prevailing horizontality of gravity-limited movement about the surface of the earth). The mere lines on a plan *are* walls in the imagination of the designing mind; their two dimensions presuming a simple extrusion into the vertical.... So although a plan is a section taken horizontally, it is a representation of the organisation of space with vertical elements.

This *Notebook*, being about walls, deals mainly in plans... plans as representations of that apparently simple and binary dichotomy between space and solid. But it is also about drawing out the hidden subtleties of plans. Someone once wrote that "architecture in general is frozen music". The 'music' of some architectural plans is far from frozen; it flows with life, movement, emotion, and poetry.

The plan of the three houses at Turn End, designed by Peter Aldington, is a complex and subtle composition of walls, some old and some new, accommodating life.

Reference for Turn End:
Peter Aldington – *Three Houses and a Garden*, 1998.

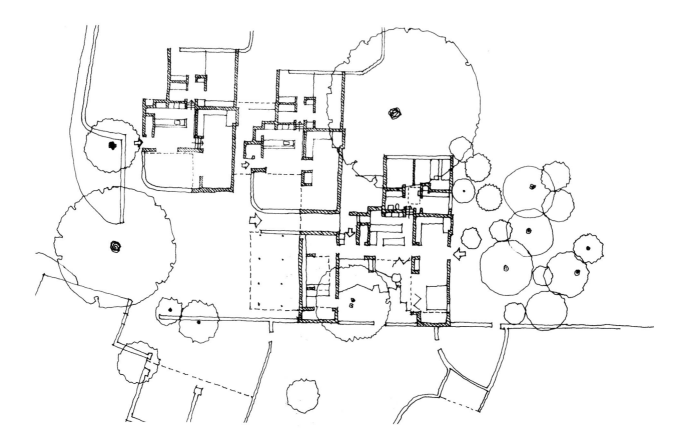

WALL AS SURFACE

WALL AS SURFACE

The 'first' walls were the walls of cliffs and caves, not conceived by a mind and constructed by effort, but *there*. They may not have been positioned with purpose, but these natural walls offer, and have always offered, architectural potential to the mind that will recognise it.

By exploring the walls of cliffs and caves perceptively, and by using them, the mind 'makes' (provokes into being by assessment and recognition) *places* (which are the 'seed' and the 'fruit' of architecture). Even in the imagination many such places can be evoked: a place to shelter from the rain and wind; a place warmed by the sun; a cool, shaded place; a place to hide from enemies; an out-of-the-way place for urinating or defecating...; a place to wash, perhaps a waterfall; a place for a fire; a place where fuel can be stacked; a place to sit leaning; a place to prop a roof; a place to climb; a high place to stand and look around; a place to hang things; a place to fix a light; a place to scratch, draw, or paint patterns and pictures, or to write out names and words; a place that can be carved into an image, or excavated into a room; a place that seems sacred and prompts worship; a place for the dead; a place that reflects the light of the evening sun, or is a screen for the flickering shadows from a fire....

Many of the uses and powers of walls must have been evident to the mind before the built wall was invented.

Walls found in the landscape are strange in comparison to built walls (or perhaps it's the other way around). The wall of a cliff has an *outside* but no inside face; the wall of a cave has an *inside* but no outside face. In both, the 'other side' of the wall is an indeterminate mass of solid matter – rock and earth. The natural wall is a *surface* between space and solid, between the space of light and air and occupation, and the solid of impenetrable matter, beyond experience, fundamentally inaccessible.... Even when the surface of a cliff or cave wall is excavated it provides no real access into the solid, only new surfaces.

The appropriation of found walls as useful surfaces was probably well established before walls were built; and there are many ways in which built walls are used as if they were found walls.

Interplay with surfaces is not marginal to our lives, it is pervasive. We depend on the ground surface fundamentally – so much so that we hardly think about how it conditions our lives. And the relationship of a wall with the ground is essential to its power in the organisation of

On the wall of the Itjari-Tjari wet weather shelter, at the base of Ayer's Rock in the centre of Australia, people drew images of things from their experience. The images mask the blank intransigence of the impenetrable wall with a camouflage of life.

Reference for Ayer's Rock cave paintings: Charles P. Mountford – *Ayer's Rock*, 1965.

space. The gravity innate to the ground, which holds us down, and conditions the verticality of the wall's construction, is the same force that makes the wall a useful instrument in the management of space.

The surface is, profoundly and simply, an interface between space that can be occupied and solid that cannot. As such it seems timelessly to have offered a metaphor for death. The family that put the body of a dead child, wrapped in bark, in a crevice in a rock face in the Carnarvon Gorge in Queensland, Australia (illustrated in *Analysing Architecture* p.43), were re-placing the child 'beyond' this surface, as a physical acknowledgement of the mortal fact. The most significant wall in an ancient Egyptian mortuary temple was that where it touched the base of the pyramid, in which was formed a symbolic doorway ('into' the solid matter of the pyramid) out through which the soul of the dead pharaoh could 'pass' to take food left by the priests (*Analysing Architecture* p.66). The wall of Lewerentz's Chapel of the Resurrection, in Stockholm's Woodland Crematorium (*Analysing Architecture* pp.82-3), may be interpreted as a metaphor for the interface between the territories of life and death; as may the wall of any tomb or mausoleum.

Being vertical (approximately or true), a wall presents its surface more immediately to the human eye than does the ground. It is also a less vulnerable situation for images. You might scrape the words 'HELP!' or 'I WAS HERE' in the sand of a beach, or idly doodle the map of an imaginary desert island, but such marks are at risk from feet, rain, and the tide... and best seen from above. On a wall, especially where sheltered, images are easier to examine and less at risk.

A wall's surface may be intransigent, but it also offers opportunities. It is the essential pre-requisite of painting, writing, graffiti... which camouflage its mortal blankness with a mirage of life: pictorial, symbolic, abstract, verbal. The wall is the precursor of the artist's canvas, the teacher's blackboard, the writer's page, the filmmaker's screen....

Over two thousand years ago the middle-eastern Nabateans began developing their capital city of Petra. They believed their gods resided in the rock, and there are many carved 'god blocks' around the city, each presumably containing within its inaccessible matter some deific djinn. Most of the Nabatean 'buildings' – tombs, houses, stores... – were carved into the rock. They

The surface of a wall is, simply and profoundly, an interface between space that we can occupy and solid that we cannot.

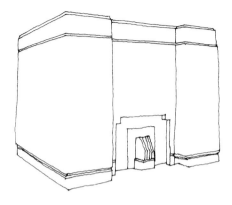

Rachel Whiteread's Ghost *(left; 1990) represents the space of a room as solid, leaving what had been the walls of the room as indefinite space. The interface between the two – space and solid – is reversed, making the space of the room fundamentally inaccessible, like a cenotaph.*

The surface of one of the walls of the Sato House designed by Team Zoo, and built in Tokyo in 1983, is a jigsaw of panels that can be removed to reveal a picture.

Reference for Sato House:
Manfred Spiedel (editor) – *Team Zoo: Buildings and Projects 1971-1990*, p.96.

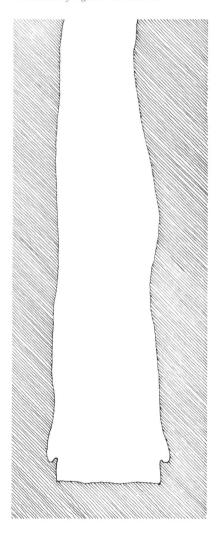

The ancient Nabateans used the surfaces of rock walls to collect rain water, which was channelled by a gutter into cisterns.

lived where water is precious, and were ingenious in engineering ways to collect and store it. Their city was (is) entered through a long, deep and very narrow ravine – the *siq* – which made the city easy to defend. When it rained, the surfaces of the walls of the *siq* ran with water which drained away, lost into the ground. So the Nabatean engineers cut a gutter into the wall, at about waist height, to channel this valuable water into storage cisterns. The surfaces of the *siq* walls acted as a collector.

The surfaces of found walls (whether they are natural or artificial is immaterial) are collectors in other ways and of other things too. They collect ephemera and records and works of art. We stick notices, posters, adverts, newspapers to them. We cover them in graffiti and slogans. We obscure them with images, symbols, icons, reliefs, ornaments, patterns... paintings dear and cheap. We carve our names and loves into them, with dates. They collect bullet and shell holes. We remember the dead on them; and the captains of sports teams; and the winners of prizes and awards and medals. We list the rules and scores of games, and the laws and punishments of society, on them. We chalk menus and offers on them, with

prices. We cover them with maps of space and schedules of time. We display trophies on them. We record the heights of floods on them. We display our wealth and identities and credentials and qualifications on them. They collect time: the wear and stains and rubbings and smells of life; cobwebs; weathering and decay; photographs and memories; the moving shadows of the day, and the passing of the seasons; dates; calendars; sundials; echoes; layers of paint and wallpaper.... Prisoners scratch the days of their sentences into them, and sketch things and people from an imagined freedom. Walls collect secrets and mottoes, signs and messages, questions and prayers.

For architects there may be some attraction to allowing the surface of a wall to

Architects might want the surface of a wall to express the way in which the wall was constructed, and the influence of the innate character of the material used...

express how it was constructed. Brick, ashlar, rough stone, wattle, logs, concrete blocks, shuttering, woven reeds, pickets, timber boards, straw bales... all seem to possess a decorative honesty.

But the surfaces of walls also invite the application of illusions to camouflage their blankness and solidity. Primitive cave or cliff drawings divert the eye from the rock surface itself, giving the mind something to interpret. Daubed or chiselled words and hieroglyphs offer something to decipher and read. Painted slogans and symbols turn the mind back from the blankness of the wall to some vital issue of po-litical conflict. *Trompe l'œil* patterns and perspectives suggest a third dimension, into the matter of the wall, which is not there. Relief carvings make that third dimension partly real. Framed pictures hanging on a wall are like windows into another world – the past, far away, paradise.... Photographic slides projected on a wall make the wall itself disappear. A mass of books ranged on shelves obscure the wall behind with the receptacles of abstract knowledge and imagination, and with the many little 'walls' of their pages, themselves covered with words and pictures. Mirrors suggest the third dimension by reflection, which

---

Reference for the Stratford Picture House, by Burrell Foley Fischer:
Jeremy Melvin – 'Superfour', in the *Royal Institute of British Architects Journal*, September 1997, pp.58-65.

The most important wall in a cinema is the one onto which the films are projected.

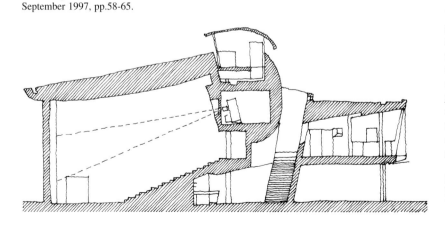

"Someone had indeed had the happy idea of giving me, to distract me on evenings when I seemed abnormally wretched, a magic lantern, which used to be set on top of my lamp while we waited for dinner-time to come; and, after the fashion of the master-builders and glass painters of gothic days, it substituted for the opaqueness of my walls an impalpable iridescence, supernatural phenomena of many colours, in which legends were depicted as on a shifting and transitory window."

Marcel Proust, translated by C.K. Scott Moncrieff and Terence Kilmartin – *Swann's Way*, 1913.

... but the surfaces of walls have, for a very long time, also been invitations for the application of illusions of space, ideas, imagination.

This is an image from the royal necropolis of the ancient Egyptian pharoah Akhenaten. It shows Akhenaten and Nefertiti mourning the death of the princess, Meketaten (not shown), who is thought to have died in childbirth. The baby can be seen being carried away.

"*Imagine an underground chamber like a cave, with a long entrance open to the daylight and as wide as the cave. In this chamber are men who have been prisoners there since they were children, their legs and necks being so fastened that they can only look straight ahead of them and cannot turn their heads. Some way off, behind and higher up, a fire is burning, and between the fire and the prisoners and above them runs a road, in front of which a curtain-wall has been built, like the screen at puppet shows between the operators and their audience, above which they show their puppets....*

"*Imagine further that there are men carrying all sorts of gear along behind the curtain-wall, projecting above it and including figures of men and animals made of wood and stone and all sorts of other materials, and that some of these men, as you would expect, are talking and some are not....*

"*... do you think our prisoners could see anything of themselves or their fellows except the shadows thrown by the fire on the wall of the cave opposite them?...*

"*Then if they were able to talk to each other, would they not assume that the shadows they saw were the real things?...*

"*And if the wall of their prison opposite them reflected sound, don't you think that they would suppose, whenever one of the passers-by on the road spoke, that the voice belonged to the shadow passing before them?...*

"*And so in every way they would believe that the shadows of the objects we mentioned were the whole truth.*"

Plato, translated by Desmond Lee – 'The simile of the cave', from *The Republic*, Part Seven, Book Seven.

changes with the position of the observer, making the illusion of space where there is solid more convincing. Cinema combines the illusion of space with the passage of time, and with a view into another world structured by a mind, telling a story.

In Alvar Aalto's conceptual design for a studio in Munkkiniemi, Helsinki (below) he included a wall on which films could be projected, for the entertainment of his colleagues.

Reference for Aalto's studio:
Richard Weston – Alvar Aalto, 1995, p.214.

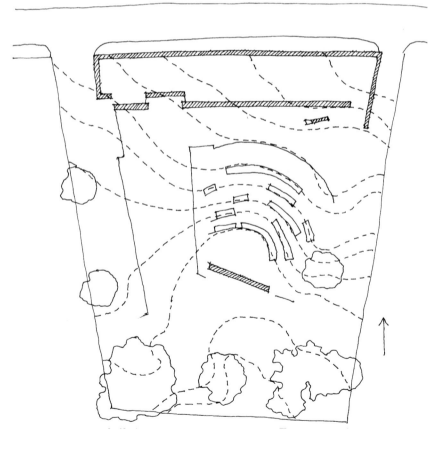

In the passage below, Rainer Maria Rilke vividly describes how the life which occupies domestic space can attach itself to the surfaces of its bounding walls.

"Will anyone believe that there are such houses? No, they will say, I'm counterfeiting. This time it is the truth, nothing omitted, and, of course, nothing added. Where would I get it from? You know I'm poor. You know that. Houses? However, to be precise, they were houses that were no longer there. Houses that had been demolished from top to bottom. What was there were the other houses, the houses that had stood next to them, high neighboring houses. Obviously, these were in danger of collapsing, now that everything next to them had been removed; for a huge framework of long, tarred poles had been rammed in at an angle between the mud of the vacant lot and the stripped walls. I do not know whether I've already said that it is these walls I am referring to. Yet it was not, as it were, the outside wall of the remaining houses (which is what one would have had to suppose) but the inside wall of the houses that once stood there. One could see the inner surfaces of these walls. On the various stories one could see the walls of rooms where the wallpaper still clung, with here and there the hint of a floor or a ceiling. In addition to the walls of the rooms, a dirty white space ran the entire length of the brick wall, and through that space crept the open, rust-speckled conduits of the toilet pipes, undulating softly in an inexpressibly disgusting, wormlike peristaltic movement. Gray, dusty traces marked the paths that gas for the lamps had followed along the edges of the ceilings; they twisted all the way around, here and there, quite unexpectedly, and entered into a hole in the colored walls, a black gap torn carelessly out of the wall. Most unforgettable, however, were the walls themselves. The resilient life of these rooms had not let itself be quashed. It was still there;

it clung to the remaining nails; it stood on the hand's breadth of floorboard; it had crept under the hints of corners, where a tiny bit of interior space still remained. One could see it in the colors that had been transformed ever so slowly over the years; blue into moldy green, green into gray, and yellow into an ancient and stagnant white that was rotting away. Yet it was also in the fresher places that had been preserved behind mirrors, pictures, and closets; for it had traced and retraced their contours, and was present in these hidden places too, with their spiders and dust, places now denuded. It was in every scrap that had been stripped away, it was in the moist bulges on the lower edges of the wallpaper, it hovered in the tattered remnants; the repulsive stains that had come into existence long ago exuded it. And out of these walls at one time blue, green, and yellow, framed by the fissured paths of the now destroyed connecting walls, the atmosphere of this life stood out – the resilient, phlegmatic, halting breath that no wind had yet dispersed. There stood the noondays and the illnesses, the exhalations and the smoke of years, and the sweat that pours from armpits and makes our clothes heavy, the fetid breath of mouths, and the musty smell of fermenting feet. There stood the pungency of urine, the odor of soot, the gray steam from boiled potatoes, and the heavy, slippery stench of fat gone rancid. The sweet and lingering smell of neglected suckling babes was there, the smell of anxiety in children who go to school, and the moist heat rising from the beds of growing boys. And much had joined this company from down below, from the abyss of alleyways, everything that had gone up in smoke; and other things had trickled down from above with the rain,

which, above cities, is not pure. And much had been blown in by the weak and domesticated housewinds that always stay in the same street, and much was there from who knows where. I've already said that all the walls had been demolished, all the way back to the rear wall –? Now, this is the wall I've been talking about all this while. You will say that I stood before this wall a long time; but I swear I began to run the moment I recognized it. For that is the terrifying thing – the fact that I did recognize it. Everything I've mentioned here I recognize, and that is why, without the slightest exertion, it runs me through: it is at home in me."

Rainer Maria Rilke – *The Notebooks of Malte Laurids Brigge* (1910), translated in D. Farell Krell – *Archeticture* (sic)*: Ecstasies of Space, Time and the Human Body*, 1997, pp.95-7.

PRIMITIVE BUILT WALLS

PRIMITIVE BUILT WALLS

"There is no need to prove in detail that the protection of the hearth against the rigors of the weather as well as against attacks by wild animals and hostile men was the primary reason for setting apart some space from the surrounding world.... Enclosures, fences, and walls were needed..."

Gottfried Semper – Introduction to 'Comparative Building Theory' (1850), in Wolfgang Hermann – *Gottfried Semper: in search of architecture*, 1989, p.199.

At Gop in north Wales, someone, a long time ago, built a wall inside a cave to create a burial chamber. This wall, from floor to roof, establishes not only an almost exactly vertical surface, but also a rectangular enclosure against the irregular surfaces of ground and rock. (After Boyd-Dawkins.)

Reference for burial chamber at Gop: Glyn E. Daniel – *The Prehistoric Chamber Tombs of England and Wales*, 1950, p.50.

To use a place that relates to a found wall is to recognise and exploit an opportunity. To conceive and create a place by building a new wall on the ground is a physical assertion of will. Architecture involves both the exploitation of opportunity and the assertion of will.

The built wall is an instrument of control and change. A wall asserts control over space, principally in the horizontal dimensions; it changes the way space is organised and can be experienced. Walls win space, and help the mind make places; they establish possession, and determine order. In asserting control over space, walls assert control over the occupants and contents of space (people, animals, plants, spirits... earth, fire, water, air...), and change

the way space can be used. A new built wall is an intrusion into the found world. It usually has a purpose; it always has an effect.

Walls affect the occupation of space in different ways. While they can include (contain), they can also exclude (shut out). They can channel movement, obstruct or prevent it. They can be used responsibly and irresponsibly, timidly and boldly, defensively and aggressively, benevolently and viciously, democratically and autocratically....

Walls may be accepted by those they affect, but they can also incite revolt. They can provide security, but they can also provoke resentment. They can give peace, but they can also take away freedom. They can

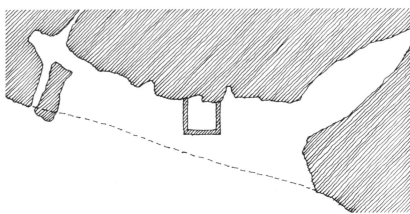

solve problems, but they can also cause conflict.

Built walls can be categorised according to their role in the management and acquisition of space. The idea for the first built wall was probably prompted by a desire to modify a place related to a found wall, adapting it better to a purpose in mind.

If you lived in a cave you might want to change it in some way to make it more comfortable and secure.

To keep out unwelcome intruders, or to make your cave warmer, drier, and more private, you might add to the walls of the cave by building a closing wall across its entrance. Depending on the material available, you might do this by weaving a lattice of branches and twigs, or hanging skins or woven fabric, or by piling up stones, or perhaps by moulding a wall in mud, that would dry in the sun. You would leave a doorway for access.

It is possible that if the rock is soft enough, you might change the walls of the cave and add to the space by excavation, creating a small niche – perhaps for a cupboard, a shrine, or a child's cot – or even carve out an additional room, for sleeping.

If you wanted to subdivide the space of the cave – perhaps to make a place for storing food or keeping an animal, or to allocate space between different inhabitants or uses, between sleeping and cooking perhaps – you might build a partition wall, again using woven branches or mud

There are various ways of amending and organising the plan of a cave. 1. It can be closed from the outside world (enemies and weather) with a wall across its mouth. 2. If the rock is soft enough, its space can be expanded, and new places made, by excavation. 3. Its interior can be divided with partitions.

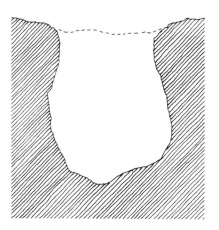
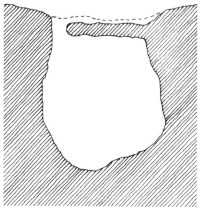
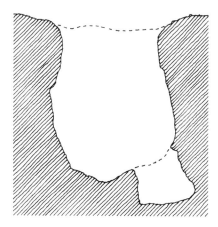

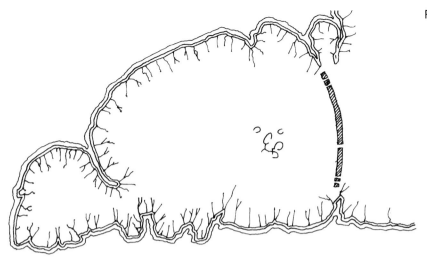

Peninsulas have, nominally, three 'walls' to the sea. This can make them attractive places of refuge from attack. In the Iron Age this peninsula on the west Wales coast – St David's Head – was adopted as a defensible place. Huts were built and, to defend it from attack from the one most vulnerable direction – the land – a wall was built, from cliff to cliff.

or piled stone, or perhaps hangings of skin or cloth.

And if you wanted to take possession of an area of ground immediately outside the entrance to your cave, perhaps for keeping an animal or increasing your sense of security, then you might build a wall outwards, into the space of the outside world, using the wall to establish personal possession of space and ground that otherwise would be available in common to everyone.

You might of course do all these things, and the resultant plan of the changed cave becomes a manifestation of the arrangement of space in relation to your existence, identity, possessions, aspirations.

In plan, each of these four kinds of built wall relates in a different way to the

4. A wall might be used to 'take possession' of space and ground outside. As a series they suggest a 'bubble' of living space emerging from inside the rock out to the space of the world. Next in the sequence would come the enclosure and the artificial cave, 'breaking free', built independent of natural walls.

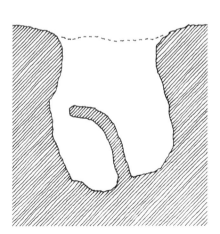

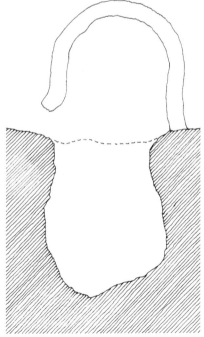

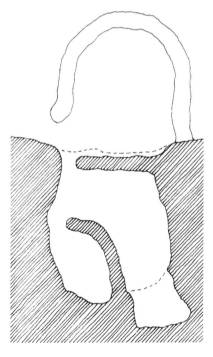

found walls of the cave and cliff. Typologically they are timeless.

Whatever their materials and methods of construction, these walls are all used to manage the ground and the zone of gravity-limited living space just above it, to draw conceptual lines in real material.

In *Histoire de l'Habitation Humaine* (translated as *The Habitations of Man in All Ages* by Benjamin Bucknall in 1876), Eugene Viollet-le-Duc suggested that some of the earliest houses were built around a fire at the base of a cliff, using the natural wall to contribute to the enclosure of space and the support of the built structure (below).

Culver Hole (below) is a cave on the south Wales coast. At some time its irregular opening was closed with a wall, to make it more useful. The wall unambiguously defines the boundary between inside and outside the cave, mediating between a small, dark interior and a bright exterior that stretches across the sea to the horizon. It was used as a dovecote.

Natural walls are barriers against enemies. Often, fortifications are walls that reinforce natural defences, creating a sheltered, superior place, commanding the surrounding landscape.

The citadel in Corte, the ancient capital city of the Mediterranean island of Corsica, uses built walls to supplement the natural defences of the rocky crag on which it sits.

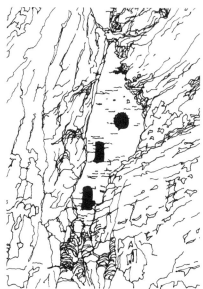

Reference for Culver Hole:
Elisabeth Whittle – *A Guide to Ancient and Historic Wales: Glamorgan and Gwent*, 1992.

The Norwegian architect Sverre Fehn has designed a number of buildings that relate, in some way or another, to natural rock walls. At Verdens Ende (World's End) in 1988 he had proposed using the walls of a large crevice between two rocks to define the space of an art gallery.

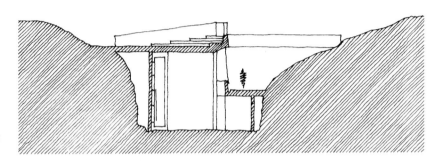

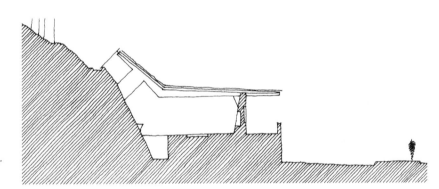

And in his design for a Museum of Hydraulic Energy at Suldal, Norway, in 1994-95, Fehn used a found cliff as back wall and support for the roof.

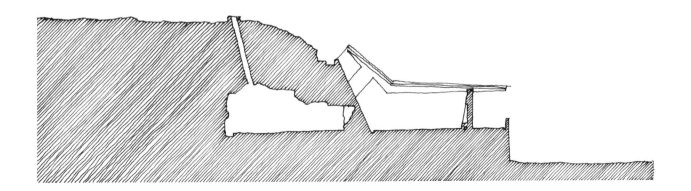

Fehn's Villa Busk at Bamble in Norway 'begins', conceptually, with a wall built on the edge of a rocky outcrop. The wall identifies and protects the space of the house. It founds both the tectonic and the conceptual structure of the house on the rock. At one end it wraps around a small swimming pool lit by morning sun. At the other end it terminates with a fireplace in the raised living room which looks across water. Along its length it is breached only by a small courtyard, between the dining room and the bedroom, and by the bridge across to the children's tower. The wall mediates between the inhabited places of the house, and the universal space over the drop.

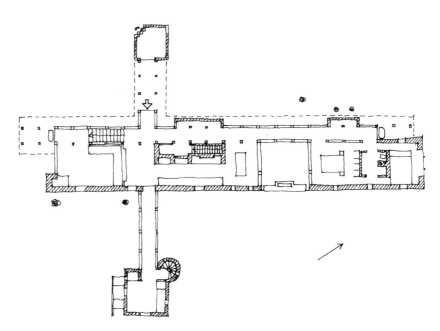

Reference for Sverre Fehn:
Christian Norberg-Schulz and Gennara Postiglione – *Sverre Fehn: Works, Projects, Writings, 1949-1996*, 1997.

The parts played in the horizontal organisation of space by the closing, partition, and enclosing wall are most directly seen in drawn plans. The powers of some other types of wall are more to do with organising space in the vertical dimension and better illustrated in section.

For example, your cave dwelling may not be at the base of a cliff, but open on to a ledge some way up. This position

So you build another kind of wall; one that will prevent you or your possessions falling over the edge. Doing more than one thing, this wall would also define an enclosure, and perhaps be used as a seat.

The same kind of wall might be built at the top of a cliff, not just as a protective kerb, but as a reinforcement of the defensive barrier the cliff provides. And maybe, if that wall is broad enough for you to walk

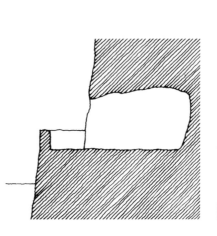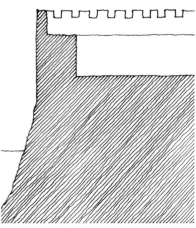

A wall might be built on a ledge to stop things falling over the edge or at the top of a cliff to reinforce the defensive barrier it provides.

might increase its privacy and security from intruders, but the precipitous threshold presents a danger to you, your children, and your animals.

along its top, then you could build another, smaller wall on its outer edge... which, if you have enemies, would shield you from their sight and missiles.

The architecture of the Acropolis in Athens depends on the power of retaining walls to establish flat ground on a craggy hill. The temples and other buildings stand on level, or almost level, platforms. And as the sanctuary was developed, over many years, more space was needed, for ceremony, and for more buildings.

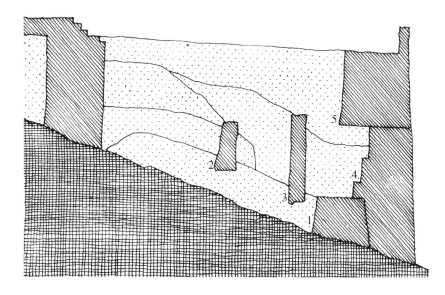

This is a cross-section through part of the Athenian Acropolis. It shows the sequence of retaining walls built over centuries successively to increase the area of approximately horizontal ground in the sacred temenos at the top of the hill. The earliest wall was the lowest of the three sections at the right of the drawing, and probably dates from more than three thousand years ago. The last portion of wall was the topmost of those three sections, built to the orders of Pericles nearly two thousand five hundred years ago. At the left edge of the drawing is the substructure of the Parthenon, the principal temple. (After Carpenter.)

Reference for acropolis substructure:
Rhys Carpenter – *The Architects of the Parthenon*, 1970, p.26.

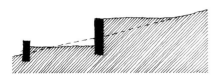

Retaining walls help make sloping ground flat, which is easier to use, or stepped terraces.

The so-called 'ha-ha' (because when one encounters it, by surprise, one is expected to utter the exclamation 'ha-ha') is a retaining wall alongside a ditch. Its purpose is to make a wall that prevents grazing animals getting into a garden and spoiling its lawns and plants, but which doesn't interrupt the view of the wider landscape from the house.

Many of the great gardens of the Italian Renaissance, built on slopes, depended in part for their grandeur and drama on the use of retaining walls to create terraces and cascades. This is the garden of the Arcadian Academy in Rome designed by Francesco de Sanctis in the early eighteenth century.

Reference for Italian Renaissance gardens: J.C. Shepherd and G.A. Jellicoe – Italian Gardens of the Renaissance, 1925.

Such walls restrain us, and our belongings, from falling over edges. Other similar walls, shown best in section, can be used to restrain, or retain, material: earth, water....

Retaining walls transform sloping ground into horizontal platforms, or a series of steps or terraces.

Although the retaining wall may, at first, seem a lacklustre invention, it plays a surprisingly important part in the mind's organisation of the world.

Flat ground, though not particularly attractive to the romantic imagination, is easier to use than a slope. Moving about on the flat is less tiring; plants grow better on flat ground because water doesn't just run away; dancing and dramatic performances work better on a flat stage; ball games are chaotic and exhausting if played on a slope; and a regular horizontal platform provides a building with a clear and incontrovertible, rather than an irregular and variable, ground datum.

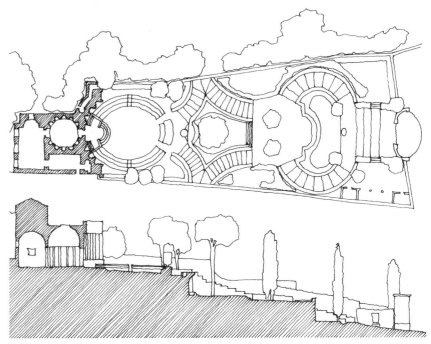

A retaining wall has the power to make irregular ground regular. It contributes to something both practical and symbolic. It is an instrument by which one of the quintessential expressions of human presence in rough landscape is established. It plays its part in asserting, physically, that the natural world can be improved according to human needs and desires, and in pursuit of some notion of perfection.

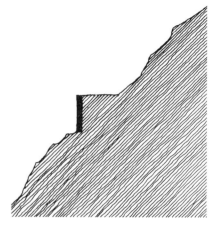

Roads and railways built along steep slopes depend on retaining walls to make level ground.

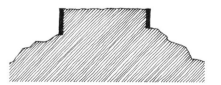

See the chapter 'Temples and Cottages', in: Simon Unwin – *Analysing Architecture,* pp.84-97.

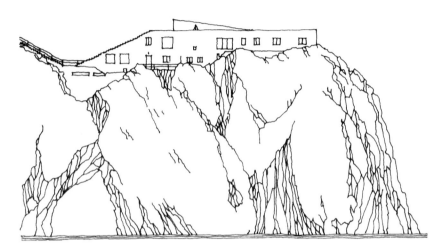

Reference for the Casa Malaparte:
Deyan Sudjic – *Home: The Twentieth-Century House*, 1999, pp.52-3.

The walls of the Casa Malaparte (above), designed by Adalberto Libera, and built on the island of Capri just before the Second World War, extend those of the natural cliffs which descend into the Mediterranean. The walls, which are red, enclose the inhabited space of the house. They also create a level platform, distinct from the craggy rocks, that is like the base of a temple, empty except for a white curved screen wall, which, whilst being sculptural, provides some privacy for sunbathing.

Because of its hilltop site, the retaining walls of the Paulus House (below) are essential to its spatial organisation of terraces, patios, and internal rooms. The house was designed by Alfredo Arribas Arquitectos Associades, and built on the south coast of Spain in 1998.

Reference for the Paulus House:
Deyan Sudjic – *Home: The Twentieth-Century House*, 1999, pp.118-19.

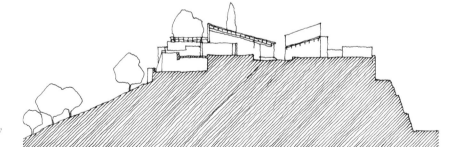

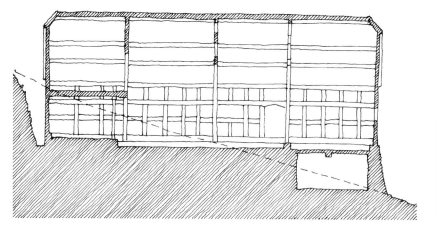

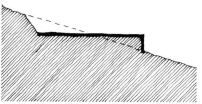

This timber-framed house in Wales (above) was built on a level platform made possible by a retaining wall towards its downhill end. The dotted line shows the approximate line of the original slope. The retaining wall also helps form a storage room under the house.

In comparison, the Eames House (below) is built on a level platform made possible by a retaining wall at its uphill side. The wall forms a backbone along the length of the house, and helps to form the courtyards between the blocks.

Reference for the Welsh platform house: Peter Smith – *Houses of the Welsh Country-side*, 1975, p.65.

Reference for the Eames house: James Steele – *Eames House*, 1994.

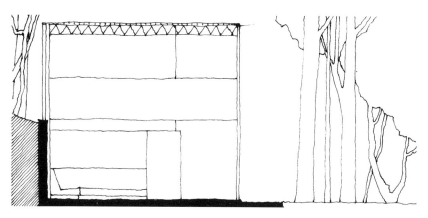

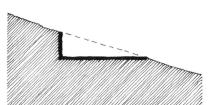

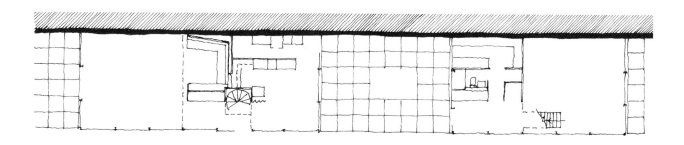

ARTIFICIAL CAVE

ARTIFICIAL CAVE

*"The cave was the original dwelling.
A hollow pile of earth was the first house.
To build meant – to gather and pile material
around empty cells for air-living-rooms."*

Rudolf Schindler, translated by Mallgrave –
'Modern Architecture: a Program' (1913), in
Lionel March and Judith Scheine – *R.M.
Schindler: composition and construction*,
1993, p.10.

It seems plausible that caves held such significance for some people long ago that, when they moved to parts of the world where there weren't any, they had to make artificial caves.

Whatever the history, creating an artificial cave involves making walls, whether by excavation or by building. The retaining wall, in converting sloping

The clearest early examples of artificial caves are ancient burial mounds with their tiny chambers, made apparently for the deposit of bones. In the attempt to give them the equivalent of the natural walls of caves, it must have seemed appropriate that the megalithic walls of these chambers should have only one surface exposed. It took great physical effort to provide the in-

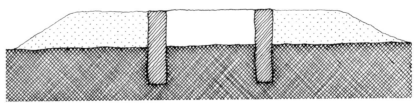

ground into flat, becomes an artificial cliff. When the aim is changed from 'making flat ground' to 'enclosing space', the retaining wall still has a key role to play.

accessible solidity and indeterminate mass of the earth around them.

Sometimes the burial mounds have a number of chambers, presumably for the

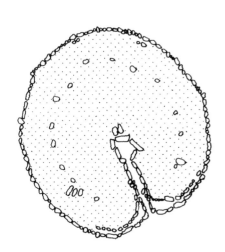

The chambers of ancient burial mounds were often made with retaining walls of large stones embedded, vertical, in the ground. A huge capstone for a roof allowed the chamber to be covered with earth, making a small artificial cave.

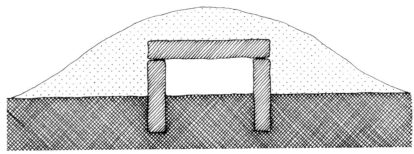

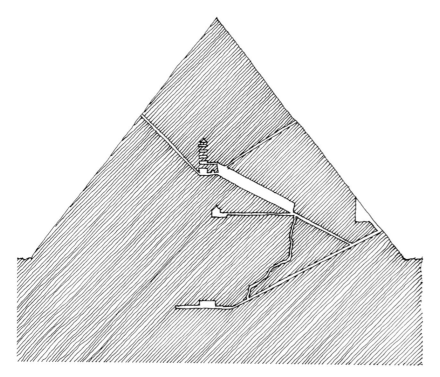

The pyramids of ancient Egypt can be interpreted as artificial cave systems, enclosed in geometrically formal mountains.

Reference for ancient Egyptian pyramids: I.E.S. Edwards – The Pyramids of Egypt, 1971.

remains of the dead of different families. These may be smaller artificial caves, off a passageway, each with its wall surfaces and surrounding mass of solid earth.

Sometimes the smaller chambers are more like rooms than caves, separated not by a mass of earth held back by the retaining megalithic walls, but a wall of a very different kind, one with two sides, two surfaces and a definite appreciable thickness; a wall with occupiable space on both sides of it – a partition wall. A wall which, instead of being a surface between the known and the unknown, is an interface between two knowable spaces. Its power is not to bound space by holding back the earth, but to stand as a divider, a means of organising compartments of space. Instead of two retaining walls holding earth between two spaces, now one wall does two things, defines both spaces, compresses the separating distance between them to the minimum.

In some artificial caves the walls of large stones are used only to hold back the earth mounded over them. In others they also divide space from space.

Reference for Bryn Celli Ddu, Anglesey, and Parc le Breos Cwm, Glamorgan (below): Glyn E. Daniel – The Prehistoric Chamber Tombs of England and Wales, 1950, p.56 and p.69.

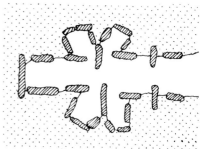

The burial chambers at Newgrange in Ireland are artificial caves constructed of megaliths and covered with large mounds of earth. The purpose was to create an internal space rather than an object. The space consists of an entrance passage and a cell. The form of the space is influenced by the 'geometry of making'. The entrance passage is formed of large vertical stones arranged along roughly parallel lines. The cell is approximately circular in plan, and roofed with a corbelled dome. In some instances the line of the passageway aligns with the rising sun at the winter solstice, allowing sunlight to penetrate into the heart of the mound.

Geometry emerges from the arrangement of great stones on the earth. Patterns and figures appear, imperfectly at first, but are progressively made more and more exact according to the predilection of the minds and eyes of those who build.

In themselves, these built walls begin to establish a distinction between the vertical and the horizontal (which perhaps was not so clear in the amorphous shape of caves themselves). Their stability depends on their verticality and integrity of construction, which begins to introduce the 'geometry of making' (*Analysing Architecture,*

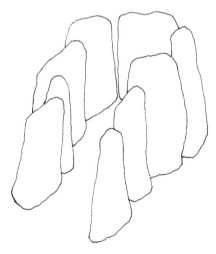

pp.116-19) with its subtle consequences for the morphology of inhabited space.

Humans are not the only creatures that build walls. Even in the nests of birds or insects – built from wax, or 'paper', or twigs and spit – the 'geometry of making' applies, and, as we see it, manifests the decisions of a mind, whether intuitively or consciously, working with material to organise space.

A built wall, as well as being practical, is also symbolic of the presence and actions of the hands that built it, and of the mind that decided it should be built. Its innate and necessary order and regularities contrast with the irregularities (and more complex molecular order) of the natural landscape, as a representation of the relationship between the mind (with its particular characteristics and concerns) and the conditions in which that mind finds itself.

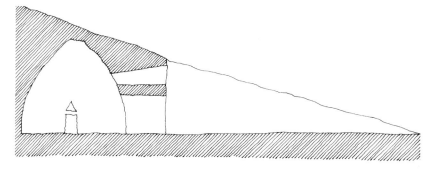

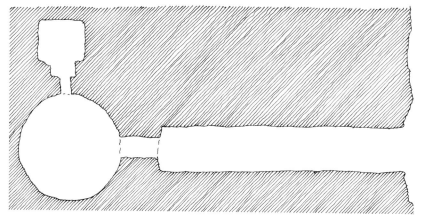

The Treasury of Atreus (right, also known as the Tomb of Agamemnon) at Mycenae in Greece is an artificial cave formed of a circular corbelled 'bee-hive' dome, and entered from a long passageway called a dromos.

The space of natural caves is amorphous, in plan and in section. There is no clear distinction between walls and roof.

In primitive artificial caves, geometry emerges, as a consequence of their having been made according to the decisions of minds, rather than according to unthinking natural forces. This geometry, of various kinds (see the chapter 'Geometry in Architecture', in *Analysing Architecture*), is evident in the layout of the walls.

Some burial chambers, maybe the earliest, are almost as amorphous as natural caves. There seems little order or pattern to the arrangement of the megaliths that make their walls, except perhaps that at least three were needed to support the capstone roof.

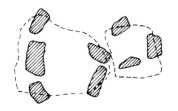

"As soon as we have learned to experience ourselves and ourselves alone as the center of this space, whose coordinates intersect in us, we have found the precious kernel, the initial capital investment so to speak, on which architectural creation is based – even, if for the moment, it seems no more impressive than a lucky penny. Once the ever-active imagination takes hold of this germ and develops it according to the laws of the directional axes inherent in even the smallest nucleus of every spatial idea, the grain of mustard seed grows into a tree and an entire world surrounds us. Our sense of space (Raumgefühl) and spatial imagination (Raumphantasie) press toward spatial creation (Raumgestaltung); they seek their satisfaction in art. We call this art architecture; in plain words, it is the creatress of space (Raumgestalterin)."

August Schmarsow, translated by Mallgrave and Ikonomou – 'The Essence of Architectural Creation' (1893), in Mallgrave and Ikonomou (editors) – *Empathy, Form and Space*, 1994.

References for: Uley burial chamber, Gloucestershire; Plas Newydd, Anglesey; Maes y Felin, Glamorgan; and St Mary's, Isles of Scilly:
Glyn E. Daniel – *The Prehistoric Chamber Tombs of England and Wales*, 1950, p.71, p.58, p.68 and p.62.

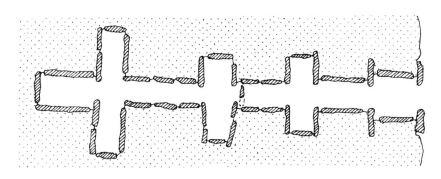

A circle implies a centre, an orthogonal space implies direction, and a sequence of spaces along an axis can imply a hierarchical relationship between them.

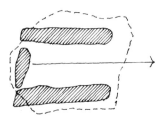

Reference for Stoney Littleton burial chamber, Somerset:
Glyn E. Daniel – *The Prehistoric Chamber Tombs of England and Wales*, 1950, p.71.

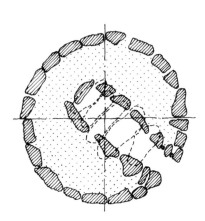

Others, perhaps later ones, show a tendency towards the orthogonal...

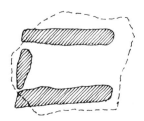

... and to the use of geometric shapes such as circles. (Below, as in the similar example two pages back, the perimeter circle of stones defines and holds in the earth of the artificial hill, which contains the artificial cave, protecting its edge.)

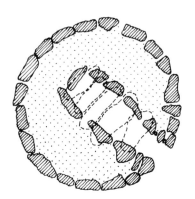

Projecting your mind, by imagination, into the minds of the people who built these burial mounds, you can speculate on why different kinds of the geometry emerged in the layout of their walls.

One explanation could be that you, as architect, might have become dissatisfied with forms that seem arbitrary, and have become aware of particular forms that appear to be special. A regular layout of megaliths may seem to you more rational; the geometry of straight lines, circles, and right-angles provides a reason for stones being placed in particular positions. In shaping a mound of a particular size, for example, there can be only one circle, whereas there are an infinite number of arbitrarily irregular shapes, not one of which can be said to be necessarily 'better' than any of the others. The circle, being unique, offers a sense of 'rightness', of authority. You might make similar arguments in favour of the straight line, alignments, and the 'right'-angle.

A second explanation might be to do with the 'geometry of making'. You might find it easier, practically, to construct a regular orthogonal cell as the artificial cave at the core of your artificial mound, than to make an irregular one.... The relevance of this explanation depends on the nature of the materials you have available for construction. If you were using components –

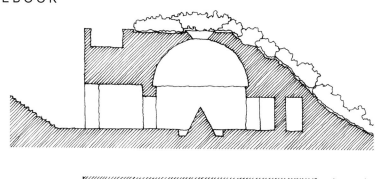

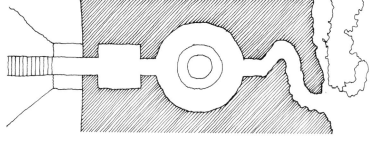

bricks and cut timber for example – which have their own geometric (rectangular) form, then it is likely that you would find it easier to build a rectangular cell. But for large irregular megaliths, of varying sizes and thicknesses, this explanation is less convincing. With this material it is more difficult for you to build a regular form than an irregular one. Your decision to make a regular orthogonal chamber requires that you find materials of roughly coordinated dimensions. The slabs of stone spanning a passageway of consistent width, for example, need to be of roughly equal length, and above a particular thickness. In this primitive instance it is not the materials that condition the form, but the mind's apparent predilection for geometric order which conditions the choice and preparation of materials.

A third possible explanation is at least as consequential as either of the others, possibly more....

It could be that you have become aware of the additional architectural powers that geometric arrangements offer in the

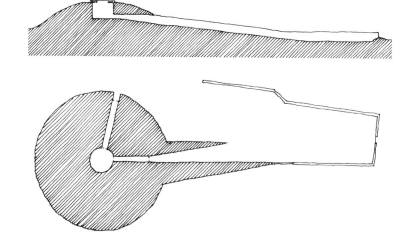

Reference for James Turrell's *Irish Sky Garden:*
Oliver Wick – *James Turrell: Irish Sky Garden*, 1992.

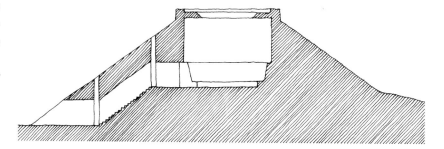

James Turrell created a series of artificial caves in his Irish Sky Garden (left), started near Skibereen in 1989. The three shown opposite are, from the top, 'The Grotto', 'The Mound', and 'The Pyramid'. Each is intended to provide a sequence of experiences which culminate in a dramatic revelation of the sky through openings in the tops of the chambers embedded in the artificial hills. (There is a map of the garden on page 131.) In each the innate geometrical order of mind-determined spaces is related to clouds through the agency of walls.

Architects in the twentieth century have created artificial caves too. This is the ground plan of an earth-sheltered dwelling built into the ground in Yorkshire by the architect Arthur Quarmby. The advantages of this technique are said to include a reduced impact on the landscape, and ease in keeping the spaces warm, because of the insulation provided by the surrounding earth. Light is allowed into the centre of the plan through a large circular rooflight, positioned over a pool of water. Poetically, the house evokes timeless relationships between dwelling and subterranean space.

Reference for Arthur Quarmby's earth-sheltered house:
Jacqui Marsh – 'Under the hill', in *The Architects' Journal*, 13 April 1977, p.687.

organisation of space and the identification of place.

A circle, for example, implies a centre; an orthogonal space begins to imply directional orientation, making a link with something distant; and a series of spaces related to an axis can suggest a hierarchical relationship between them.

Here is the begininning of an awareness of the power of walls, as instruments of the mind, to overlay a framework of (perhaps magical) order on the world. It can send a thrill down the spine to think of what follows from these primitive examples. The axes and alignments evident in ancient temples and medieval cathedrals, Renaissance houses and modern atria, can be traced back to the experiments of prehistoric builders discovering the powers inherent in special alignments of walls.

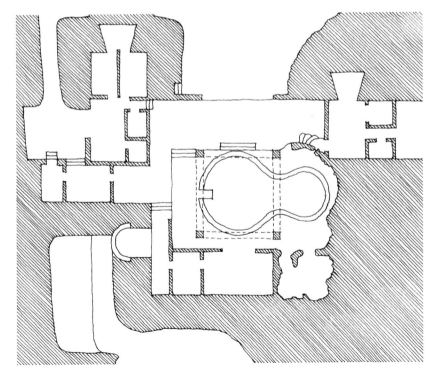

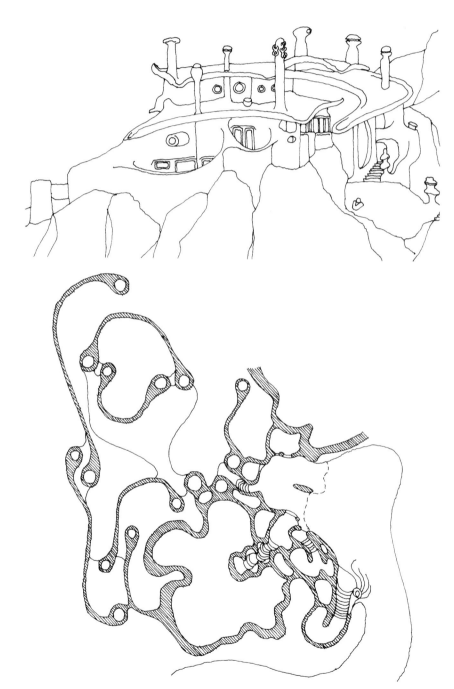

Amancio d'Alpoim Guedes described a house he designed in Zimbabwe as having been conceived as a metaphor for a woman. It is also irregular in form, like a cave, drawing the age-old analogy between the earth and the mother, the cave and the womb:

"Ladies and gentlemen, I present my first habitable woman; a vigorous, personal, erotic, obscure, suprafunctional, suburban citadel. The castle of the Queen of Sheba. A fortress for a princess. My own ideal palace being built on instalments. An anthropomorphic wonder-house. An incredible white and luminous construction melting into a low-veld koppie. A round-eyed house of cavernous passages built into the rock gaps, of swinging walls finding their own levels, of fluid ceilings and floors, of many stairs and steps, with lights staring and pouncing out of ceilings and walls; a house with a baby-house inside her. A pregnant building. A doll's house with secret and hanging gardens."

Reference for Amancio d'Alpoim Guedes' house in Zimbabwe:
John Donat (editor) – World Architecture 2, 1965, pp.176-7.

NAKED CAVE

NAKED CAVE

Conceptually, if not historically, the next stage in the evolution of the power of walls comes when the artificial cave is left uncovered with earth, naked to light and sight. Then the cell acquires an external form as well as its internal space. And the walls, partitions now between a specific inside they define a hidden, secret chamber, occupiable only perhaps by death. They are visible, surfaces presented to the outer world as well as to the interior. The walls are no longer interfaces between space and the unknowable, but between zones for life: an 'inner' private life and an 'outer' pub-

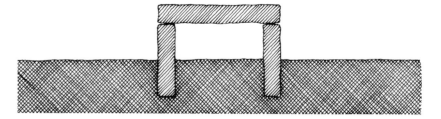

and a general outside, cease to be experienced as single surfaces between occupiable space and inaccessible solid. Each acquires an extra external surface, with different aspects and prospects, various possibilities and potentials.

The walls of this naked cave can be more accommodating to life. No more do lic, social, political life. They can be penetrated, not just by a subterranean passageway, but with openings which allow views from inside to outside, and light to penetrate the interior.

Underground, the artificial cave acquired new characteristics, born of having to be made, but also of the contributions,

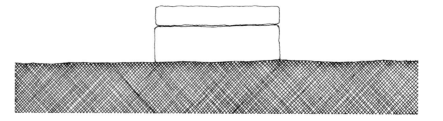

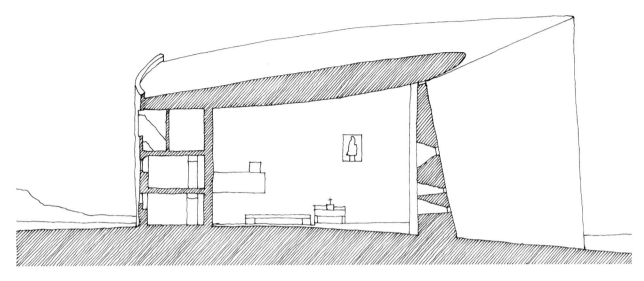

predilections, perceptions of the mind making it. Left outwardly exposed, the walls acquire yet more powers.

The space of the 'cave' is no longer merely a cavity isolated in an indeterminate amount of solid matter, and approached down a passageway long enough to suggest an almost complete separation from the everyday world, but a space which relates to other spaces. The walls of the naked cave are no longer retaining walls – interfaces between occupiable space and inaccessible matter – but have now become partition walls between an 'inside' and the general 'outside'. The consequence of this, conceptually, is that the inside becomes more a place for the living, rather than the dead, and as such more one piece in a

The pilgrimage chapel at Ronchamp, designed by Le Corbusier, and built in the 1950s, with its apparently heavy roof bearing on sloping slabs of wall, resembles an ancient dolmen. As such it is an artificial cave...

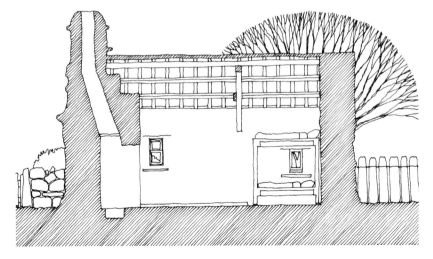

The interior of a cottage is like a cave...

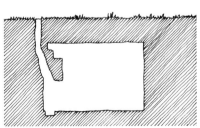

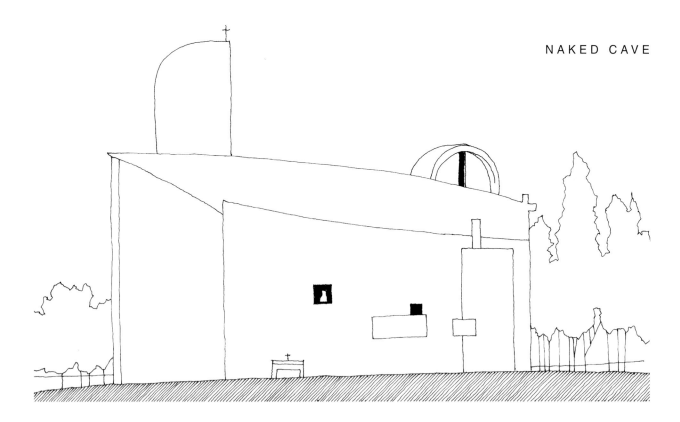

... but one exposed to sight and light. As such the building is a sculptural form set in the landscape, as well as one enclosing an internal space. One's experience of the two is very different. From outside one is able to look at the building as an object. Inside, one is surrounded by the building and experiences the interior as a place.

Reference for the chapel at Ronchamp:
W. Boesiger – *Le Corbusier: œuvre complète (Volume 5) 1946-1952*, 1995, pp.72-84.

patchwork of living spaces – inside and outside – rather than a place set apart, in the unknowable.

The walls of a naked cave, spatially, do at least two things at once. Each of their two faces contributes to the identification of place by delimitation. One delimits the outside realm, the other the inside, making a place set apart from everywhere else, but

one which has the potential for a variety of linkages with its adjacent outside.

Those linkages are made possible by the relative thinness of the walls. The passageway of the chamber tomb can be reduced to a doorway, with the possibility of almost instant transition from outside to inside and inside to outside. Windows, for light and ventilation, impossible in the

... but its walls present a face to the outside world.

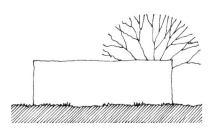

The cottage is an artificial cave surrounded by space and light and life, rather than by earth.

chamber tomb, become possible. And although one's attention may well be focused on the walls' contribution to the making of an internal space, they also hold the potential of contributing to 'positive' outside places, with their own identities of use, ambience, and environmental character.

Some burial chambers show the beginnings of direct relationships between inside space and 'positive' outside space. In these the cell is positioned near to the edge of the earth mound so that the passageway can be reduced to a doorway, and

a forecourt is made for the performance of funeral rituals.

Le Corbusier's chapel at Ronchamp has an internal space that is in some ways reminiscent of the inside space of a dolmen (megalithic burial chamber). It also has an outside space for worship, with its own altar and pulpit, focusing on the east wall of the chapel (on the left in the drawing). The figure of Mary in the small window in the wall can be turned to face services inside or outside. The curve of the wall, convex inside and concave outside, together with

Some burial chambers show attempts to make a relationship between the cave-like inside space and a 'positive' outside space, probably for funeral ceremonies. This is Tinkinswood burial chamber in south Wales. Instead of a passage entrance there is a forecourt, carved out of the mass of the earth mound, with immediate access into the chamber through a small doorway..

Reference for Tinkinswood burial chamber:
Elisabeth Whittle – *A Guide to Ancient and Historic Wales: Glamorgan and Gwent,* 1992, pp.10-11.

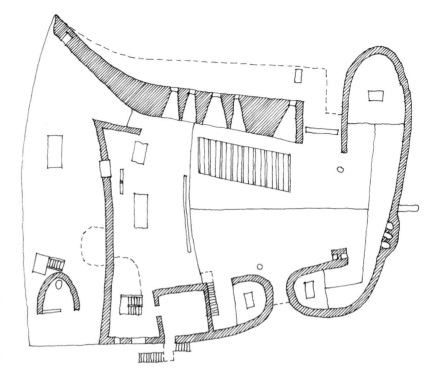

Holes can be made in the walls of the uncovered artificial cave for light and air. Access is easier, more immediate; no long entrance passages are needed. There is more immediate interaction between internal and external space. Le Corbusier's chapel at Ronchamp has an external space for services, alongside the east wall, as well as the internal (right).

The cottage (below) has various 'positive' external spaces – the roadway by the door, the small yard adjacent to the chimney wall, and its garden.

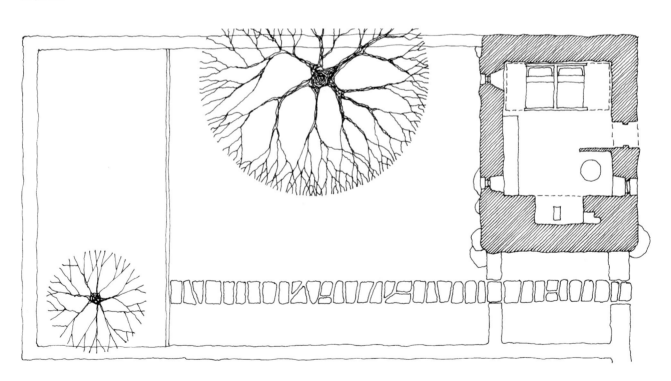

the overhang of the heavy roof, acknowledge this 'positive' outside space.

The cottage, even if a simple single cell, comprises a matrix of inside and outside spaces. The example on the previous page has at least three positive outside spaces relating to three of its four walls:

the pathway outside its door; a small wood yard adjacent to the chimney wall, and its garden, enclosed by its own walls (which also bound fields).

Through being made of vertical walls supporting a horizontal roof over a horizontal

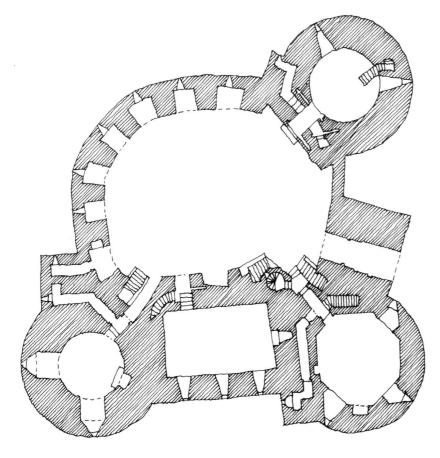

Sometimes walls are so thick that passing through openings in them can seem like going through a passageway. Some of the walls of Castell Coch, outside Cardiff at the entrance to one of the south Wales valleys, are thick enough to contain passageways and stairs.

Reference for Castell Coch:
David McLees – *Castell Coch*, 1999.

floor, the subterranean artificial cave made a clearer distinction between the horizontal and the vertical than was apparent in the natural cave.

When, in the naked cave, the space inside becomes more accessible to both life and light, that clarity and simplification of infinite directions into an orthogonal six becomes more apparent. Now the constant downward pull of gravity is no longer the only clearly directional force acting on the occupant. There emerges from the darkness a clear differentiation between floor, walls and roof.

Other, more subtle attractions affect life within, and outside. And the literal burden of the roof, which never affected the form of a natural cave, but which the walls of the artificial cave acquired in its subterranean state, continues to impinge on and affect the relationships between the walls of a naked cave, conditioning its spatial organisation.

The mind has also begun to be aware of the subtleties attaching to the composition of walls in horizontal space, the effects of positioning walls in different relationships to each other: the ability to

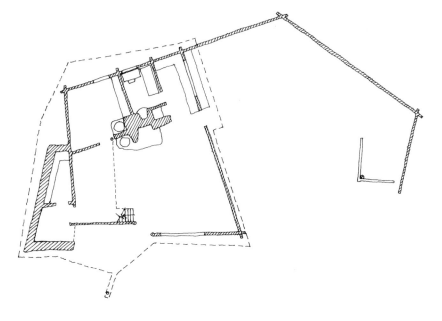

The thinness of the log walls of Ralph Erskine's scout hut at Drottningholm, Sweden, built in 1953, allows an immediacy of relationship between inside spaces, and between the inside and the positive outside space enclosed by a palisade.

Reference for Erskine's scout hut:
Peter Collymore – *The Architecture of Ralph Erskine*, 1994, pp.60-1.

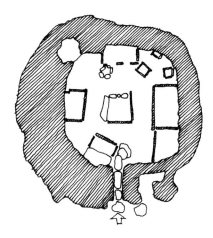

The forms of naked caves are influenced by and reinforce the geometries of architecture. This house (above) at Skara Brae on Orkney is a roughly circular loop enclosing space. Other buildings reinforce the six directions – forward, back, left, right, up, down – by the orthogonal form of their walls.

focus space; to establish and relate to specific directions – forward, back, left, right; north, south, east, west; sunny, shady, morning, evening; to channel routes; to halt movement; to contain; to exclude; to create hierarchies; to juxtapose secret private spaces with open public ones; to exploit the mystery of views from one accessible space into another inaccessible one; to establish linkages; to divide; to incarcerate; to protect; to hide; to reveal; to create mystery; and so on....

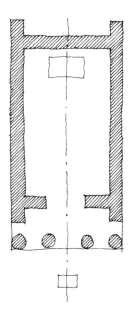

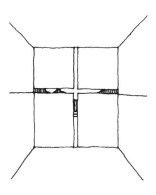

Reference for Tadao Ando's Chapel of the Light (above):
Masao Furuyama – *Tadao Ando*, 1993.

Reference for Skara Brae (top):
Michael Parker Pearson and Colin Richards – 'Architecture and Order: spatial representation and archaeology', in *Architecture and Order*, 1994.

Reference for the 'Chapel of the Great Cross' (right):
Friedrich Achleitner (introduction) – *Walter Pichler: drawings, sculpture, buildings*, 1994, p.93.

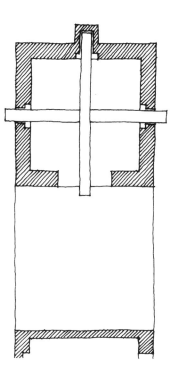

EXPRESSION

EXPRESSION

The appearance of a wall is expressive of its coming into being, and of the conditions of its existence. A wall may express many things: about its purpose; about its location; about the way it was designed and built; about the influence of material and gravity on its construction; about the skill of the person who built it; about the attitudes and intentions of the mind that conceived it; about the aspirations and status of its owner; about the way it is maintained (or neglected).... The mind that designs a wall has control over some of these. To others it must respond. To some it has to concede.

A stone wall can express a lot. Most obviously it is explicit about the way it was made... of stones found in the fields... large enough to bond together as a structurally stable wall... but not too large as to be impossible for one or two people to lift and place in position. The mind that conceived the wall was probably intent on keeping animals contained on a particular area of ground, or on keeping them from spoiling growing crops, or on asserting possession. It achieved this with the expenditure of time and effort rather than money, unless the mind employed the hands and skill of others to build the wall it conceived.

The design of this wall is hard to separate from its construction. Maybe there was an idea in a mind before it was made real, but the form of the wall emerged and

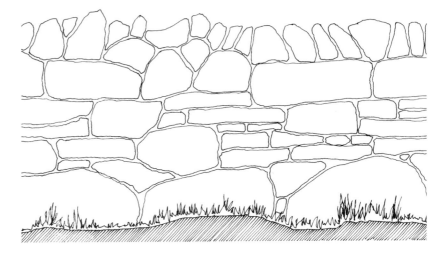

was finalised during, and as part of, the process of building. The wall's thickness, height and appearance were influenced by the character of the stone available in the field. Smaller, rounder stones have to be piled into a thicker wall (and with battered, sloping sides) than flat, laminated stones (slate, for example) which bear on each other neatly and in stable courses. Polygonal stones have to be assembled like a jigsaw without a pre-determined master plan. More subtle assembly is needed where there is a variety of different sorts of stone. In this way the form of the wall is intimately related to the character of the stone available, and hence the geology of the land on which it is built...; a wall can express something innate about the landscape in which it stands.

But walls in regions with similar geology and stones might be built in different ways, maybe according to different

The shapes of available stones influence the form and character of the walls that can be built from them.

Round pebbles or boulders, which are difficult to balance one on top of others, have to be piled into a heap...

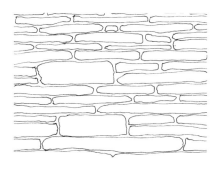

... whereas flat stones can be laid in courses to make a wall with vertical sides.

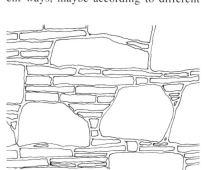

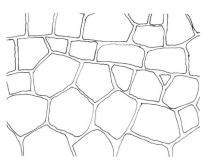

Polygonal stones can be put together like a jigsaw... but one without a master 'picture' to follow.

Such walls express a subtle interplay between the shape of the available stones and the judgement and decisions of the mind that builds them.

78

Similar-shaped stones can, however, be laid in different patterns. Different regions might have different traditions for laying stone.

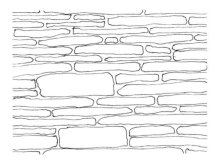

Flat stones can be laid in horizontal courses...

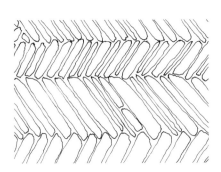

... or they might be stacked diagonally...

... or even laid in vertical courses.

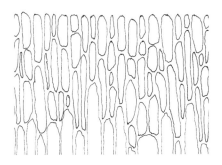

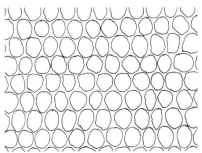

Pebbles, or flints, which are round, need mortar to hold them together as a vertical wall.

traditions of construction. In three regions – all with large, thin, flat stones – field walls might vary in character: the traditional technique in one might be to course stones horizontally; in another to stack them into diagonal chevrons; and in another to place them in courses that are vertical.

In stone walls there is a vital interplay between the innate character and shape of the stones available, and the conception of possibilities of construction by the mind that builds. Possibility and conception must be in accord for the production of a successful wall, but there may well be more than one way to do it.

The existence of a wall attests to the existence of the people who built it. The wall draws out a line of boundary across the land, determined by their decisions. It describes, literally, their parcelling out of ground. The wall does this by being. Its character, however, may express the skill and possibly also the character of the person who built it. The skills of dry-stone walling are ones of judgement and craft, and these may be individual. One can imagine that, even using the same material, two dry-stone wall builders might produce walls with characteristic differences born of their different ways of making judgements and of placing one stone upon others. Stone walls can express the personal building styles of their makers.

The selection and positioning of stones can express something of the thoughts and attitudes of the designing/building mind, and of that mind's appreciation of techniques for achieving better structural stability or perhaps neatness. Large rectangular stones might be used as quoins, at edges and corners, to increase structural strength at these vulnerable parts of the wall. A course of smaller stones, laid

The ends and corners of stone walls might be built of larger, longer, squarer stones, called quoins, to increase the strength of this vulnerable part of the wall.

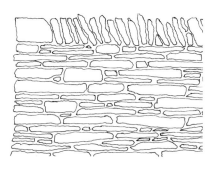

The top of a stone wall might be finished in a special way, maybe with smaller stones stacked vertically.

The character of a wall might express the skill, or lack of skill, of its builder. Its collapse might express something about the state into which the building or estate of which it is part has been allowed to fall.

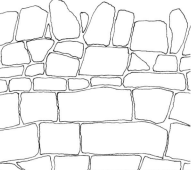

The way a wall is built might express something of the personality of the person who built it.

vertically, might be placed along the top of a wall, to finish it.

Walls can express the skill of a builder, but they can also express ineptitude or neglect. A hurried mind or unskilled hand might pile stones together chaotically, with neither reason nor understanding. And broken, unrepaired walls can express something about the commercial health of the farm whose fields they define.

Walls can also express technical skill and effort. The Incas of central America built walls of massive stones fitted precisely together (below), perhaps rubbing one on another to achieve an exact fit.

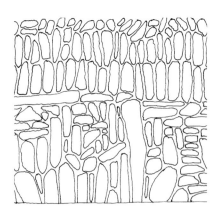

The stones in this wall (above), arranged both horizontally and vertically, illustrate something of the pleasure the builder must have gained building it.

Inca walls were built with huge stones, not squared, but fitted precisely against each other. These wall express something about the organisational and technical abilities of the people that built them.

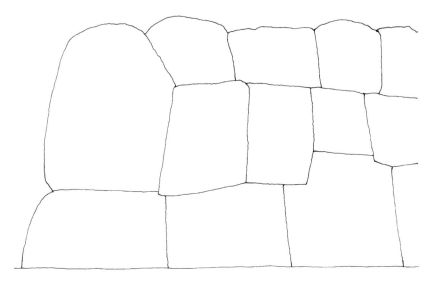

Minds can decide to do things with walls that are not dictated by their function, or by the demands of structural stability or construction. The stonework on the right is decorated with small stones pushed into the mortar joints, in a way which can make one smile at the simplicity of the idea.

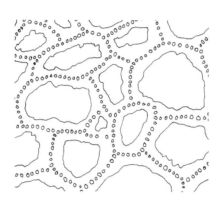

Andy Goldsworthy uses stone walls in his land-art sculptures. In this example (below) he has built the trunk of a fallen tree into a dry-stone wall.

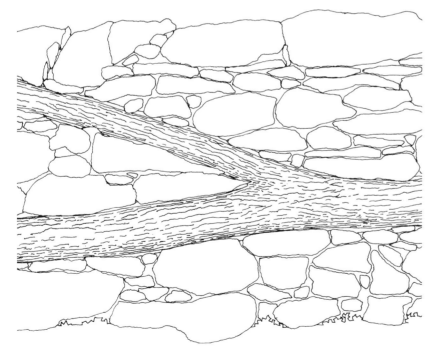

Andy Goldsworthy uses stone walls in his land-art sculptures. In this one he has built the trunk of a tree into a dry-stone wall, in a way which challenges you to think about their relationship. The wall becomes a visual poem about the differences in nature between stone and timber.

Reference for Andy Goldsworthy's land-art sculptures:
Andy Goldsworthy – *Wood*, 1996.

Walls must be structurally stable to survive. That stability too can be expressed in the way they are built. The bonding of stones – that is, the way they overlap each other in the courses, obeying the general rule of laying one stone always on at least two in the course below – ties the stones of the wall together, making it less possible for it to fall apart.

When there are openings in walls, the structure might be more complex.

These two windows, side by side in a wall in Jerusalem, are provided with wedge-shaped voussoirs which make a flat arched lintel over them. The builder seems also to have felt it necessary to try to reduce the weight pressing on these voussoirs, or perhaps at least to provide a safety measure in case of their failure, by building a 'relieving' arch into the wall above. In this the wall expresses two complementary structural ideas (the arch is actually redundant).

The wall over this pair of windows in Jerusalem expresses the two structural ideas of: 1. a set of wedge-shaped stones (voussoirs) forming a flat arch; and 2. a relieving arch, thought to reduce the load bearing on the voussoirs.

Reference for Jerusalem walls: Salomon Moshé – Urban Anatomy in Jerusalem, 1996.

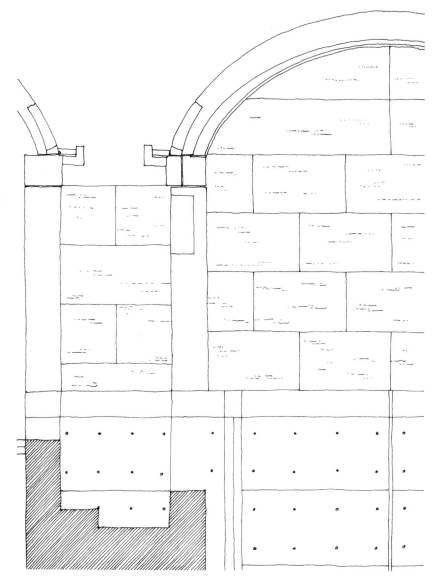

Louis Kahn expressed a smilar idea in the brick walls of the Indian Institute of Management in Ahmedabad, India (below), which he designed in the 1960s. A structural idea – the brick arch embedded in the wall, spanning between the upturned ends of a concrete tie beam, used elsewhere in the building over actual openings – is expressed decoratively in the body of the wall.

And the end walls of Kahn's Kimbell Art Museum (right) in Fort Worth, Texas, built in the late 1960s, clearly express the concrete components of the structure, and differentiate between the concrete plinth on which they stand, and the infill travertine walls that close the internal spaces.

Some walls are very old, and may have been altered many times in response to changing needs and perhaps fashions. As well as expressing the way in which they were made, and something of the in-

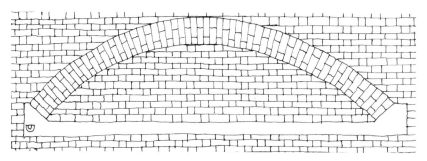

The walls of Kahn's design for the Indian Institute of Management (left) express a structural idea.

And in the end walls of his Kimbell Art Museum (above) different materials are used for the structural frame, the plinth, and the infill panels.

Reference for Louis Kahn:
Hisao Koyama – *Louis I. Kahn, Conception and Meaning*, 1983.

nate influence of the materials on their construction, such walls may also express their history. This wall, in the old walled city of Jerusalem has been changed many times. There are the remains of arches over openings that no longer exist, and obviously

This wall in the ancient walled city of Jerusalem expresses something of its history, with changes layered upon changes.

Reference for Jerusalem walls:
Salomon Moshé – *Urban Anatomy in Jerusalem*, 1996.

newer openings – doors and windows – with their own arches or lintels. The stonework is in different styles of construction, sometimes rough but original, sometimes rectangular stones built in regular courses, sometimes rough infill with stones wedged in to close openings that are no longer needed. The result is a wall which seems to tell a story of its past; not a complete story but one that stimulates the imagination to interpret the changes that have been made over the centuries, and to evoke the lives of those who made them.

The layers of history evident in the wall in Jerusalem may have happened without conscious intent, products of repeated desires for change without the expense of radical rebuilding. When Carlo Scarpa re-furbished the Castelvecchio in Verona during the 1960s (below) he wanted to allow the building as a whole, including of course its walls, to express their layers of history, with his own amendments being one more layer added to those of the past.

Other minds concerned with building walls with stone seem to have been more intent on reducing the contribution of the innate character of the stone, or the construction technique, or the effects of time, to a minimum. Their concerns seem to have been to make a wall which might be said to be 'perfect'. This involves chiselling stones to perfect rectangular blocks, standardising their sizes so that courses can be even, or even making every block identical in size so that the joints of the wall

Carlo Scarpa, in his work at the Castelvecchio in Verona, wanted the building to express its layers of history, including those he was adding.

Reference for Carlo Scarpa's work at the Castelvecchio:
Richard Murphy – *Carlo Scarpa and Castelvecchio*, 1990.

Cutting stone into rectangular blocks can make building a wall easier, and the result stronger. It reduces the character contributed by the irregular shapes of the stone, and the personal judgement of the person making the wall.

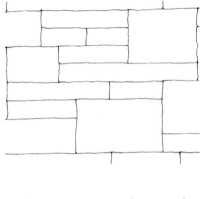

The urge for 'perfection' is furthered by standardising the sizes of stone so that courses can be regularised, even if the course are not all the same height.

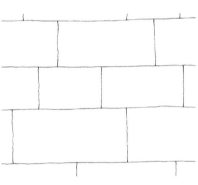

In some walls the heights of the courses are made the same.

And the 'perfect' wall, devoid of any geological, regional, traditional, personal... expression, consists of rectangular stone blocks all of identical size. Such a wall expresses a desire for mathematical and impersonal exactitude.

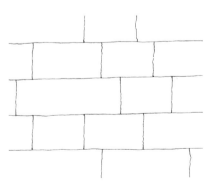

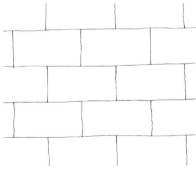

are regular and equal. Such walls leave no space for the expression of a style of construction related to a particular character of stone, or region, or to the personal skill of a specific builder. They express something at the opposite end of a spectrum from personality or the relation of character to a particular place or culture or tradition. They express a desire for universality. This is the sort of wall that can be built anywhere, and which cannot be tied to a specific place, material, culture, person....

Bricks are regular-shaped building blocks, standardised in size to make wall building easier and results more predictable. They may relate in character to the place where their material originates – for example, London bricks are made from London clays – but they are also easy to transport, and brick walls do not always express local character or traditions of con-

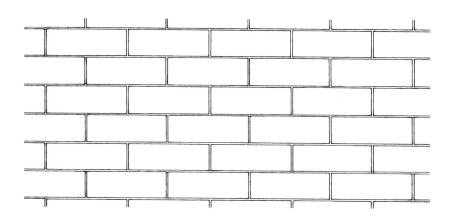

struction. Nor is there as much scope in a brick wall for the personal judgement or skill of the mason as there is in building a rough stone wall.

The ancient Romans made long, square-faced, bricks, which could be stacked diagonally into what was called *opus reticulatum* (right).

Generally bricks are oblong blocks, of sizes which can vary, but which are of a convenient size to be picked up with one hand during building. Despite their standardisation, there are things that brick walls can express. They can express the 'softness' of hand-made bricks or the sharp-edged hardness of machine-made bricks. A wall built of re-used broken bricks might express poverty and a need to avoid expense, or it might express a desire not to waste re-usable material, or a carelessness

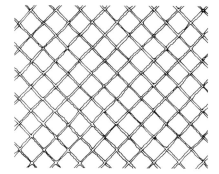

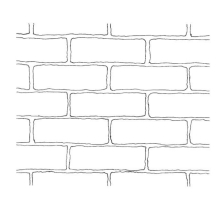

In slightly different ways from stone, brickwork can be expressive of the quality of the material used and the ways in which it is put together. Different sorts and sizes of brick have been used in different periods of history and parts of the world. The precision of work, or the use of broken bricks, can be expressive of attitude and of resources.

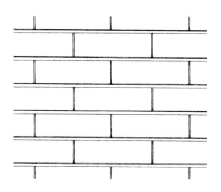

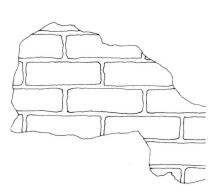

In 1977 Susan Kaiser Vogel built a small brick maze called Blue Flame *in the courtyard of the Frederick S. Wight Art Gallery in Los Angeles. (For illustration, see page 136.) She described the process of building, and explained how she wanted the brickwork to be expressive:*

"I built the structure without mortar. I put mastic butter between each brick, so that you could see only brick to brick, like the grid of a human nervous system rather than a visible mortar system. The process of putting up the work was very meditative."

Reference for Blue Flame:
Jan Butterfield (editor) – *The Art of Light and Space*, 1993, p.207.

Reference for Aalto's summerhouse at Muuratsalo:
Richard Weston – *Alvar Aalto*, 1995, pp.114-21.

about appearance.... A clean, well-maintained brick wall expresses something different from one that is dirty, damaged, dilapidated.

Bricks can be built into decorative patterns (right), expressing a desire to transcend the merely pragmatic and utilitarian. In his summerhouse, built in 1953 on the island of Muuratsalo, Alvar Aalto played with different patterns of brickwork (below), expressing in the wall a spirit of experiment, and producing a surface which attracts attention, and decorates the small courtyard of which it is part.

The bricks in walls may be arranged to decorate or achieve aesthetic effect, but

some architects have managed to arrange bricks in ways which suggest a philosophical or even a religious intent.

In his two churches – St Mark's, Björkhagen (1956-60), and St Peter's, Klippan (1962-66) – the Swedish architect

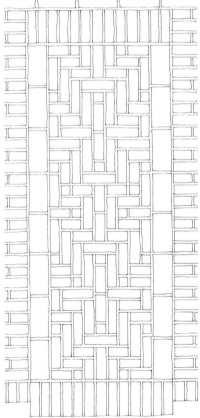

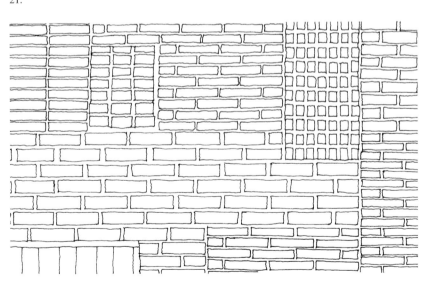

Sigurd Lewerentz used bricks in particularly idiosyncratic ways. In St Mark's he used bricks of irregular shapes, put together in a way that was not regimented. It is as if he wanted to respect the individuality of each brick and the contribution it made to the wall as a whole. He expressed the cohesion of the wall by allowing the mortar

Reference for Lewerentz's churches:
Claes Dymling and others – *Architect, Sigurd Lewerentz*, 1997, pp.146-63, and
John Krause – *Two Churches*, 1997, p.84.

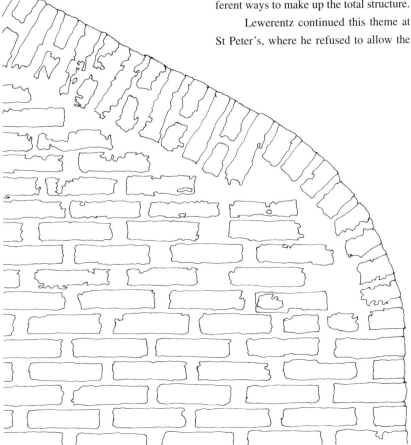

of the joints to smear over the edges of the bricks. Perhaps the brick walls are a metaphor of the society of human beings in the church, with different people, each with their different characters, suited to different contributions, playing their part in different ways to make up the total structure.

Lewerentz continued this theme at St Peter's, where he refused to allow the bricklayers to cut any of the bricks. Each brick had to remain whole, as if they had to be treated as individuals. Again the mortar was allowed to smear over the edges of the bricks (using a process called 'bagging', in which the mortar is rubbed smooth rather than pointed with a trowel). Each brick, uncut, had to play its part as well as it could in the scheme of things. At joints and intersections, and where the wall was irregular, this led to some strange joints... places where there seemed to be more mortar than brick.

Lewerentz's brickwork, a collaboration between his mind – the contributor of the philosophical idea – and the skills of the bricklayer, is some of the most expressive brickwork ever achieved in building. The notion that a brick might 'die' and hence be useless if one cut it in half is both poignant and ludicrous, but the suggestion that a wall can be a metaphor is powerful. It reminds one of some of the writings of architectural theorists in the nineteenth century who championed Gothic and vernacular architecture, as expressive of human personality and individuality, against the style of Classicism, which was criticised as subjugating individuality to uniformity and formulaic rules. There are many places from which apposite quota-

The ruined walls of a medieval castle are expressive of a period of history long past, and of the political and social structure associated with the times.

tions could be taken, but probably one of the most appropriate is John Ruskin's chapter 'The Nature of Gothic' in his book *The Stones of Venice*, written around 1850. The chapter can be read as an essay on its own, and contains many passages relevant to architecture as an expressive medium, especially in its relation to the culture and society of human beings as makers and thinkers. Here are just a few quotations that seem pertinent to the way Lewerentz seems to have been thinking when his churches were being built:

"Christianity... recognized, in small things as well as great, the individual value of every soul. But it not only recognizes its value; it confesses its imperfection, in only bestowing dignity upon the acknowledgement of unworthiness."

"Rather choose rough work than smooth work, so only that the practical purpose be answered, and never imagine there is reason to be proud of anything that may be accomplished by patience and sandpaper."

"...since the architect, whom we will suppose capable of doing all in perfection, cannot execute the whole with his own hands, he must either make slaves of his workmen in the old Greek, and present English fashion, and level his work to a slave's capacities, which is to degrade it; or else he must take his workmen as he finds them, and let them show their weaknesses together with their strength, which will involve the Gothic imperfection, but render the whole work as noble as the intellect of the age can make it."

There are many more passages, from this long chapter, that could have been selected to illustrate Ruskin's attitude to architecture, building, and design.

The front wall of Inigo Jones's Banqueting House, built on Whitehall in London during the beginning of the seventeenth century, wears its decoration like a dress. It was one of the first buildings in Britain using the Classical style. Its front wall expresses allusions to the confidence and humanism of the Renaissance, and its own reference to the heroic humanism of classical antiquity.

Reference for Inigo Jones's Banqueting House:
John Summerson – *Inigo Jones*, 1966.

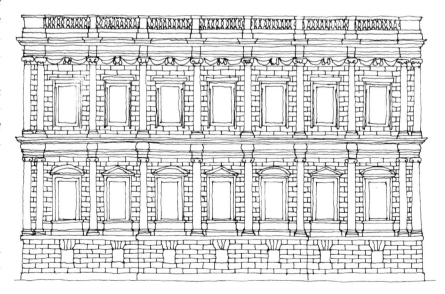

The elevations of Newgate Prison in London expressed the power and inescability of the law and the exercise of its punishment.

Reference for Newgate Prison:
Reginald Blomfield – 'The Architect of Newgate', in *Studies in Architecture*, 1905, pp.73-90.

Of course architects can use walls to express many other things besides what Ruskin might call 'truth to materials', or 'truth to the skill and humanity of the workman'. Architects have often used walls as canvases on which to project ideas and allusions. Inigo Jones, in the façade of his Banqueting House, wanted to express something very different from the sentiments Ruskin wished to champion some

three and a half centuries later. He introduced the revived Classicism of Renaissance Italy to Britain, bringing with it evocations of the heroic culture of ancient Rome and the adventurous spirit of contemporary Italy.

The Debtors' Gate of Newgate Prison (left, now demolished) in London drew on the association of Classicism with ideas of control and discipline, but also, by use of a gigantic scale in its stonework and deeply recessed joints emphasising the solid mass of each individual block of stone, added a poetry of the imposition of the weight of law and punishment, creating an elevation expressing incarceration and an almost total absence of even the merest hint of mercy or leniency. Notice that where in a domestic or civic Classical elevation there might have been swags of foliage carved in stone, i.e. in the space above the door, here there are chains and manacles... symbols of imprisonment. The door beneath seems mean and small, with miscreants entering like mice through a mousehole in this massive stone wall, made insignificant and worthless by comparison with the power of the state.

Many buildings use such associations, particularly the association of the Classical style of decorating architecture with ideas of respectability, discipline, reliability, honour, dignity, nobility, power, wealth.... The walls of this Renaissance palace in Rome, the Palazzo Caprini (also known as the House of Raphael), express something of the status and aspirations of the person for whom it was built. Even the

stratification of the façade reinforces the essential ideas of nobility. The base of the building is built in strong-looking rusticated stonework, supporting the more refined columns and entablature of the upper, noble floor, where the main living apartments are situated.

The expressive language of classical architecture can take on a life of its own, eclipsing the space-defining roles of walls. In his fantasy village in north Wales – called Portmeirion – Clough Williams-Ellis gathered together fragments of redundant buildings, including parts of this 'Gloriette', which, although it looks like a complete building, is just a decorated wall.

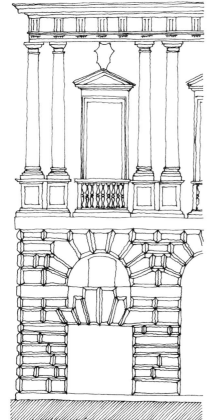

The Gloriette at Portmeirion, designed by Clough Williams-Ellis, is a decoration in a garden. Though one can stand on the balcony, it is not so much a complete building as an ornamented wall.

Reference for the Gloriette at Portmeirion, north Wales, by Clough Williams-Ellis: Richard Haslam – *Clough Williams-Ellis*, 1996, p.98.

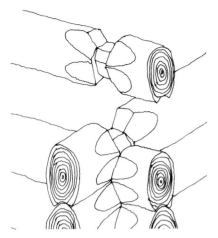 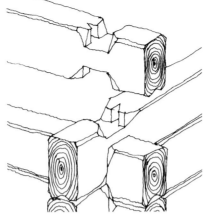 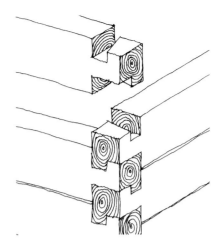

The expression of construction, even in a simple log wall, can be quite sophisticated. These examples are from Norwegian log houses.

Reference for Norwegian log houses: Drange, Aanensen and Brænne – *Gamle Trehus*, (Oslo) 1980.

The same concepts as have been applied above to stone walls and to brick walls can also be applied to walls built from timber. They might express clearly the ways in which they were constructed, and the innate characters of the materials used, such as in a wattle screen made of woven twigs or laths, or a wall made of notched logs, not squared, and without even their bark removed.

Such walls can, as with stone or brick walls, express the concerns, aspirations, resources, traditions, and skills of the people who make them.

Walls built of timber can be expressive. Their appearance might depend on the type of timber that is available, or the techniques developed by a particular group of people, or on the aspirations and intentions of the those who decide on how they should be built.

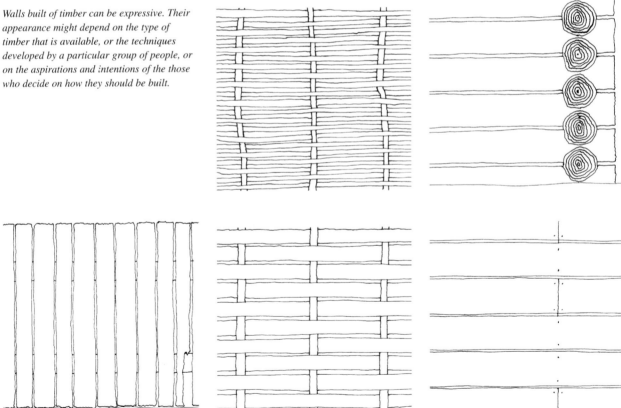

Similarly, timber walls can be built in ways that express pride in craftsmanship, or assertions of gentility and wealth. The walls of a timber-framed house might be built, to use Ruskin's words, "so only that the practical purpose be answered", producing a pattern which, though stimulating to the eye, is born primarily of utility and pragmatism.

Or the mind responsible for the wall might want to make special efforts to manipulate the appearance of the wall, decorating it, as in the example to the right in which the diagonal bracing in each panel of the frame has been carved into decorative shapes, to express aspirations that claim to be 'higher' than utility.

Both these gables are from Welsh houses. In the one on the left the pattern of the timber frame is dictated primarily by a pragmatic attitude to making a wall. In the example on the right, there has been a conscious attempt to decorate the wall by carving the bracing in each panel of the upper floor.

Reference for Welsh timber-framed houses: Peter Smith – Houses of the Welsh Countryside, 1975.

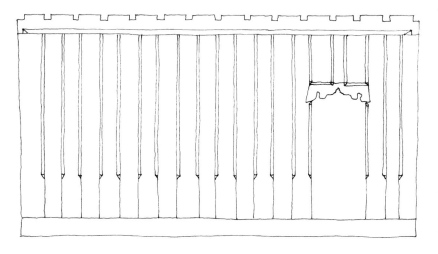

The drawing on the left shows the internal screen wall in Trewalter, Llangors, Wales. It was constructed of vertical planks set into a cill plate and head plate. The planks were chamfered and smoothed to express politeness.

Timber-framed walls may be simple and straightforward, dictated by the nature of the material used, the practical need addressed, and the demands of structural stability. These factors must be taken into account, but the designer of a wall may wish to do more, to decorate and arrange the components of the wall in ways that seem to stimulate the aesthetic sense, or perhaps evoke allusions either to an admired period in the past – such as the Middle Ages – or to some presumed moral principle. The drawing on the right is from a timber-framed wall in France, recorded by the nineteenth-century architect A.W.N. Pugin, who believed that medieval buildings expressed moral superiority over buildings designed in the Classical style.

Reference for Pugin's records of French timber-framed buildings of the Middle Ages: A.W.N. Pugin – *Details of Ancient Timber Houses of the 15th & 16th centuries...*, 1836.

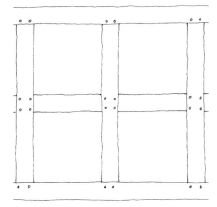

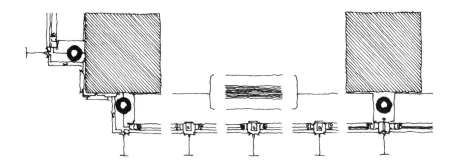

Sometimes, perhaps because of the forces of fashion or of the desire to assume the trappings of status, people have tried to invest cheaper materials such as timber with the appearance of brick or stone.

The drawing below shows the construction of a wall in what are called 'mathematical tiles'. These are made of fired moulded clay and can be hung on battens fixed to a timber frame to give it the appearance of being a brick wall.

And the corners of the timber building on the right have been fitted with timber 'quoin stones' to give it some of the appearance of having been built in stone.

Such practices, which are evidently possible and have at some times been popular, challenge Pugin's and Ruskin's assertions that 'truth to materials' and 'truth to craftsmanship' possess an unassailable moral virtue.

Mies van der Rohe designed walls that appeared, particularly at their corners, to be supported on steel structures. He manipulated the detail to enhance the expression of technological exactitude and sharpness.

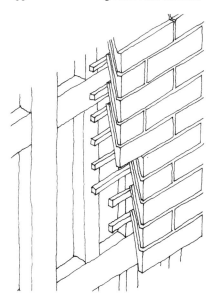

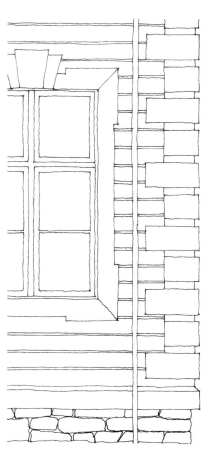

Some builders have been intent on making one material look as though it is another. Usually the aim has been to make a cheap wall look like an expensive one, expressing a desire to impress at the expense of honesty. In these examples a timber-framed wall is given a skin of false brickwork, and another is given pretend 'quoins'.

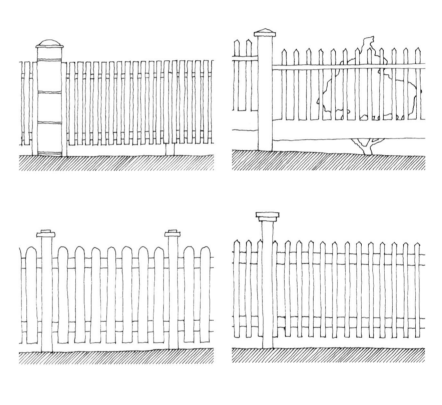

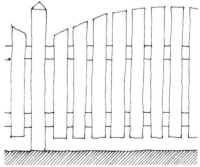

The residents of Seaside, Florida, a new town designed according to the principles of Contemporary Traditional Urbanism (as set down by Andres Duaney and Elizabeth Plater-Zyberk), are required to demarcate their plots with wicket fencing. They may express difference, if not individuality or personality, by varying the design of their fence within stated parameters. The whole expresses the framing of individuality within the authority of a rule system.

Reference for Seaside:
David Mohney and Keller Easterling (editors) – *Seaside: making a town in America*, 1991.

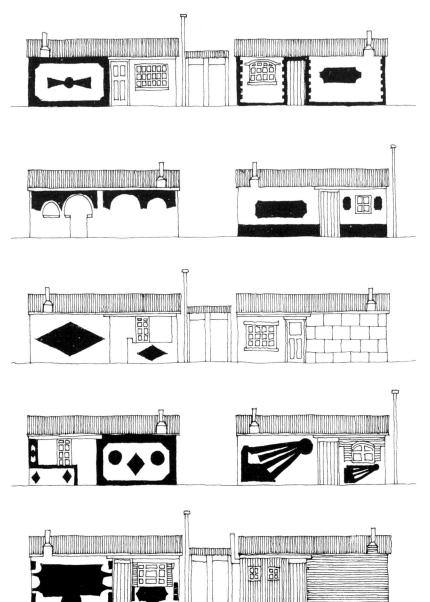

These are elevations of some of the two thousand houses that were in the Western Native Township, South Africa, in the 1960s. At the time Amancio d'Alpoim Guedes wrote of them:

"In the township all the houses are two-faced. Their first faces were blank, dark and alike. Their first faces were drawn in offices according to the rules of minimum standards, regimentation, numbers and sums. Their second faces were invented by the people alive within them. These masked houses shout and speak in an unselfconscious, spontaneous language of great vitality. These tough, boisterous, bright signs and forms metamorphosed the dusty and bleak township into a colourful and vivid playground."

Inhabitants were asked various questions, such as "Why did you decorate your house?" Answers included:

"The house was made of plain unattractive bricks and I had to change the appearance to satisfy myself."

"I did not want my house to look like the other houses in my street."

"I told the builder a tree design would have a great significance with the people that used to come for prayer at my house."

"I was a schoolteacher and so wished to enhance my status."

"I wanted to show originality in my taste."

"I wanted to direct friends who did not know my home so as not to get lost."

"I wanted to show typical Tswana designs."

"I wanted something that would look modern instead of the decorations we do in the farms."

John Donat (editor) – *World Architecture 2*, 1965, pp.184-93.

Earlier in this Notebook *it was suggested that, because drawing and painting originated on the natural walls of cliffs and caves, paper could be considered to be an artificial and portable 'wall'. Until recently architects have used paper for preparing their designs. In this situation there is an intriguing relationship between the portable 'wall' of the paper and the actual wall being designed. Sometimes actual walls are treated as if they are pieces of paper with designs on them, and built as such.*

The African walls opposite are treated by their owners as pieces of paper on which they can make patterns. This house (right) is a design for a town house and studio by Charles Rennie Mackintosh, made around 1901. First one can see that the intended wall, if built, would have expressed clearly the individual style of this particular architect. But second, one can also see that Mackintosh treated the design of the wall, whilst obviously taking into account the internal arrangements in the disposition of the windows, as being like a composition on paper.

Reference for Charles Rennie Mackintosh: Jackie Cooper – *Mackintosh, Architecture,* 1977.

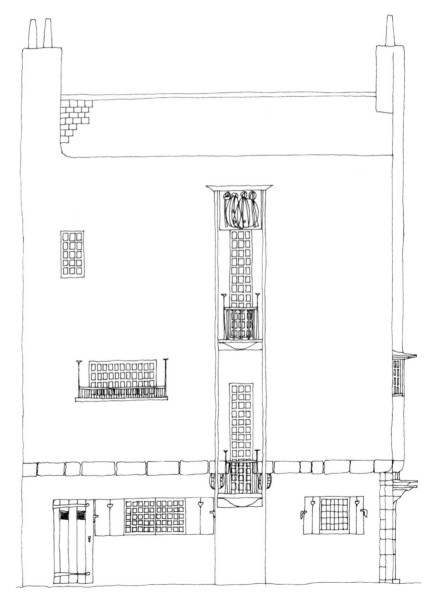

Interior designers of the De Stijl movement in the 1920s wanted to challenge and disrupt orthodox and traditional ways of decorating walls. They treated them as canvases on which they painted abstract compositions intended to dissolve the apparent solidity of the wall into rectangles of different strong colours with varying 'depths' and textures. This is the design for a wall in the Café Aubette, by Theo van Doesburg, dating from 1927.

Reference for De Stijl interior design: Carsten-Peter Warncke – *De Stijl 1917-31,* 1991.

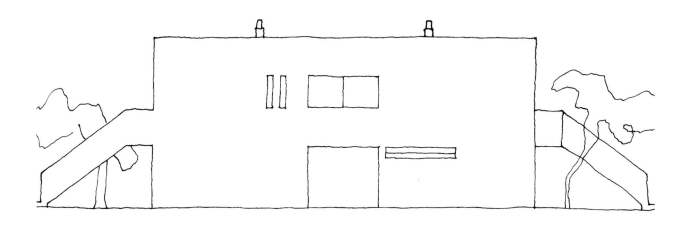

In his house designs of the 1920s Le Corbusier adopted an uncompromising attitude to the decoration of walls – they had none (below, and opposite page). He reasserted the primary role of the wall as a demarcation of space rather than as a canvas for decoration.

Nevertheless there were ways in which Le Corbusier did treat walls as if they were built pieces of the paper on which he drew out their designs. He believed in the aesthetic authority of what he called 'regulating lines', which he composed geometrically on paper, and which he allowed to dictate the proportions and arrangements of his elevations (right).

Later, when Le Corbusier had developed the his system for the dimensional organisation of buildings – the 'Modulor' – he would also use some parts of the walls of his buildings as a billboard on which to advertise his system (below right).

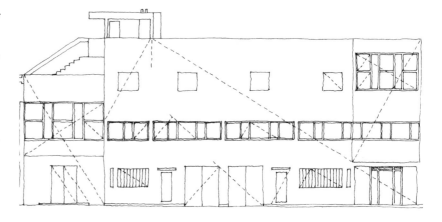

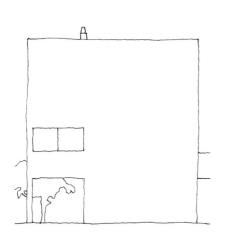

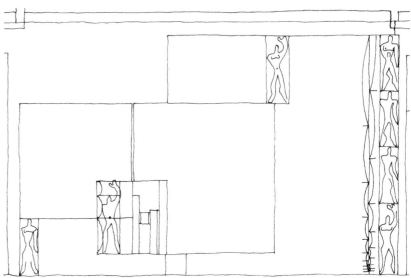

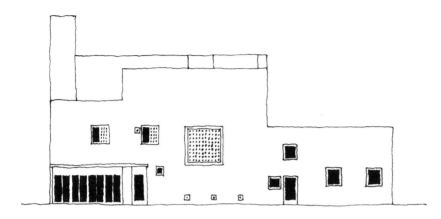

Whereas the front wall of the house Luis Barragán built for himself in Mexico City expresses little more than a desire for an almost monastic privacy, and perhaps a prioritisation of the lighting of the internal spaces in special ways...

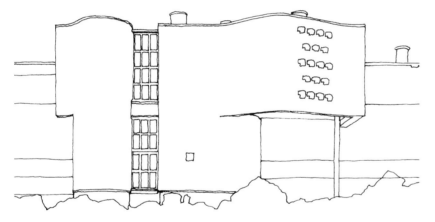

... Ralph Erskine engaged in an architectural use of simile in making the front wall of this cardboard factory look like a piece of paper.

Walls have been used in giving identity to buildings in many ways... maybe by association (as in the case of using a style from the past), or by metaphor or simile (as in the case of Erskine's cardboard factory), or perhaps by providing a ground for labelling (in words), as in this supermarket designed by the architectural design firm SITE. In this example they do something else too: they use the elevation as a medium for expressing a sense of humour.

The use of walls for 'telling jokes' has been a characteristic of the work of SITE. One of their designs for Best supermarkets had its wall peeling away at the top, another had a section at the corner that pulled out (literally) to make the entrance. In this one, which dates from 1989, part of the wall is apparently crumbling into a pile of bricks on the canopy over the entrance.

And in this building, the Paz Building in New York (1983), SITE 'tear' away part of what appears to be a traditional wall to reveal the glass wall of a 'modern' building.

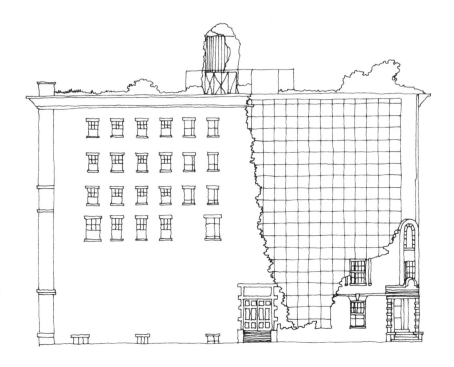

Reference for SITE:
James Wines – *SITE*, 1989.

Reference for Luis Barragán:
Raúl Rispa (editor) – *Barragán, the complete works*, 1995.

Reference for Ralph Erskine:
Peter Collymore – *Ralph Erskine*, 1994.

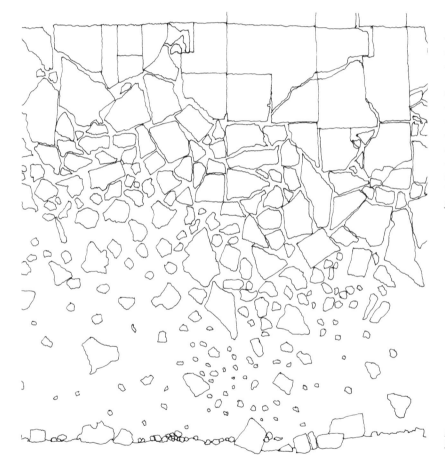

This is part of a project called 'Frozen Archaeology' designed by SITE in the 1980s. It presents the image of a wall disintegrating, not from the top down, but from the bottom up. The fragments of broken wall are, of course, supported on a backing wall which is structurally secure... so the disintegrating wall is only an image of a wall rather than a wall itself. The wall is a poem about disintegration... about the breaking up of the regular panels, traces of which one can just about see remaining at the top of the drawing. The representation of movement, falling, is frozen...

Reference for SITE:
James Wines – *SITE*, 1989.

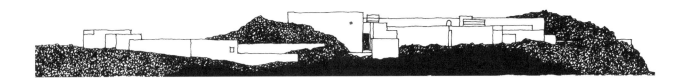

The presence of a wall on the surface of the earth expresses the existence of the people who decided it should be built, those who designed how it should be, those who built it, and those who use it. As such, a wall can be expressive of people's insecurities, aspirations, possessiveness, defensiveness, assertiveness, aggression, status, imagination, knowledge, skill, technical understanding, locality, resources, culture, traditions, interests, allegiances, recreations, activities.... All these might be expressed in the physical fabric of the wall itself, but the wall also expresses its own purpose – the demarcation and enclosure of space.

Concentration on the expressive potential of the fabric of walls can reduce awareness of the powers of walls in expressing the organisation of space, and the identification of place. One of the reasons why some architects have refused to decorate their walls, or even to show how they were built, has been to return concentration to the roles walls play in the manipulation of space.

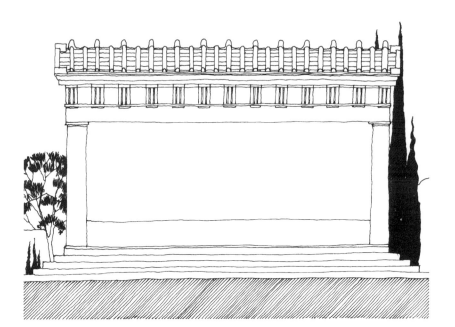

The side wall of a temple is a canvas for decoration, but its primary role is to enclose the space within.

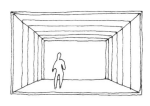 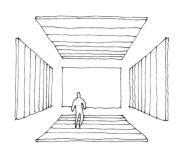 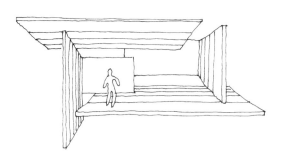

In his book The Modern Language of Architecture (1978), *Bruno Zevi illustrated the way in which the destruction of the simple box of space could return architects' attention to the ways in which walls could manipulate space in subtle ways.*

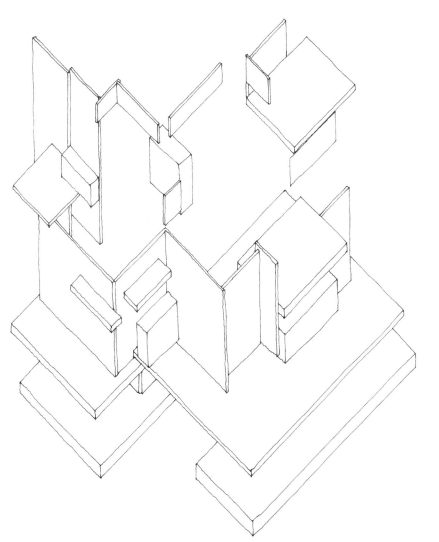

The drawing on the right illustrates an exploration of spatial organisation using planes, by Theo van Doesburg, called 'Counter Construction'. (1924).

Reference for Counter Construction:
Carsten-Peter Warncke – *De Stijl 1917-31*, 1991, p.171.

ENCLOSURE

ENCLOSURE

"Hang out our banners on the outward walls;
The cry is still, 'They come'; our castle's strength
Will laugh a siege to scorn."

William Shakespeare – *Macbeth*, Act V Scene v

Just as one may consider the naked cave, conceptually, as emerging from the ground, so too one can think of the enclosing wall as breaking free of the natural wall of the cliff.

'Lassoing' a piece of ground by building a wall around it is, before all else, an assertion of possession. The mind that

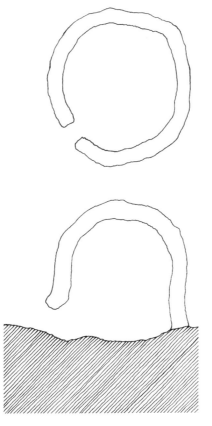

decides to build the wall wants to make clear that this piece of ground belongs to it, is under its control. Such assertion can have various motivations: a desire to keep and protect; fear of incursion, theft, attack; aggression; acquisitiveness; assumption of rights of possession; to establish clarity of land rights and boundaries.... The wall carries these purposes: manifests them in effective physical reality, and represents them symbolically.

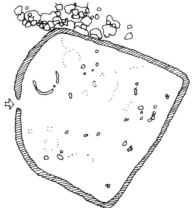

When people built a wall around a piece of ground on Winnall Down (and there are millions of like examples across the world) they were taking possession of, humanising (or beginning the process of humanisation of) a patch of raw natural landscape. The wall marked and bounded ground and space that thereby became special. It provided a certain 'inside' (a home) to mitigate the infinite uncertainty of the 'outside'. It protected their houses (eight), perhaps from animals, perhaps from human enemies. Maybe it also kept their domestic animals, and small children, close to home.

An enclosing wall establishes, incontrovertibly, a defined area of ground,

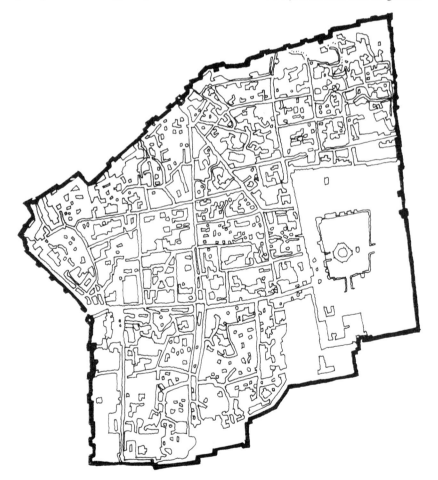

The enclosing wall of the ancient city of Jerusalem demarcates its definite boundaries. Inside is very different from outside. Inside is specific, outside is anywhere (or everywhere else). Inside is an organism of apparently chaotic life, but actually ordered in its complexity; outside is actual chaos. The walled city is a symbol and manifestation of humanity.

"... long before (city walls) were military erections, they were a magic defence, for they marked out from the midst of a 'chaotic' space, peopled with demons and phantoms, an enclosure, a place that was organized, made cosmic, in other words, provided with a 'centre'. That is why in times of crisis (like a siege or an epidemic), the whole population would gather to go round the city walls in procession and thus reinforce their magico-religious quality of limits and ramparts."

Mircea Eliade, translated by Rosemary Sheed – *Patterns in Comparative Religion*, 1958, p.371.

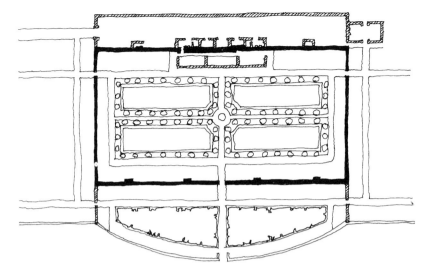

The high protective walls of a kitchen garden create a special microclimate that helps propagation and growth. They also enclose a special world....

Reference for kitchen gardens:
Susan Campbell – *Charleston Kedding*, 1996.

"The world walls made a vast square, the type of all perfect gardens and cloisters, the enclosure four-square, in which, according to Avesta, man was first placed. The square paradise of Yima, where men were saved from the flood."

W.R. Lethaby – *Architecture, Mysticism and Myth*, 1892, p.62.

"A Marxist would maintain that the walled enclosure as an image of the good place where high civilisation is in flower is nothing but a mystification of the facts."

Seamus Heaney – 'From Maecenas to MacAlpine', in John Graby (editor) – *150 Years of Architecture in Ireland: The Royal Institute of the Architects of Ireland 1839-1989*, 1989, p.70.

which is the prime basic element of all terrestrial architecture. It separates a place from everywhere else. It does this physically and psychologically.

There are innumerable examples of significant places that begin, conceptually, with an enclosing wall. In all of them the walls assert the separation of a place from the rest of the world, for a variety of different reasons. In many of them the enclosing walls do other things too.

The examples that follow illustrate some of the numerous powers of enclosing walls.

Enclosing walls define a space and portion of the earth's surface. They can protect something sacred from the profane world outside, and by concealing it enhance its fascinating mystery. They can bound private property, distinguishing it from common land. They can defend possession. They can relate to the natural topography of the ground, but when they are made geometrically orthogonal they can align directions, either in relation to the movement of the sun through the sky, to the imposition of political and military discipline on the surrounding landscape, or

in relation to some near or distant sacred location. They can define an area for a game, performance, or a symbolic contest, reinforcing the internal directions inherent in those activities, and concentrating their sounds. They can protect from enemies, keep property safe, and prevent escape of prisoners or kept animals. They can provide a frame for thought and debate. They can establish correspondences, suggesting a datum to which other things, within or without, may relate. They can alter the climate in a space, making it possible to make a more luxuriant garden inside than would be possible outside. They can establish the domain of a person, a family, a town, a city, even a whole nation. They can hide a place of pleasure, even debauchery, from the eyes of envious onlookers. They can sanctify ground where the dead are buried. When orthogonal, they can define the 'square world' of human beings, and identify a symbolic 'centre', occupied perhaps by the 'seat' of the most important person in a society or deity in a religion. They can encapsulate heaven, or some earthly representation of paradise. They define the human.

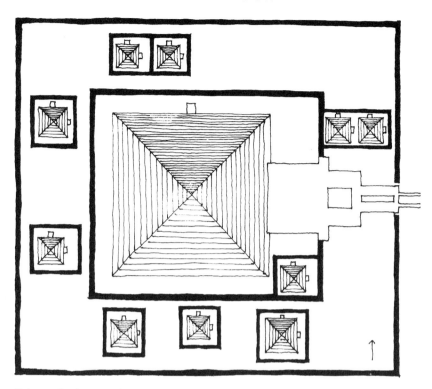

Reference for the pyramid complex of Sesostris 1:
I.E.S. Edwards – *The Pyramids of Egypt*, 1972, p.162.

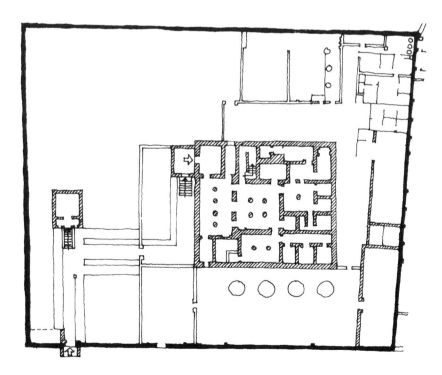

The pyramids of ancient Egypt (which can be interpreted as geometrically perfected artificial hills containing artificial caves) were surrounded by enclosures defined by walls. This is the pyramid complex of Sesostris 1 (c.1900BC). Presumably the enclosure walls were intended to prevent ordinary people approaching close enough to the pyramid to threaten its sanctity, and also to underline its separation from everyday life. The wall, built to a height well above eye-level, would also have meant that the pyramid could only be seen from a distance, as something 'there', rather than close-up as something 'here' and tangible. The enclosure wall seems to have been an essential component of pyramid architecture. In this example there are two, concentric walls. The central enclosure contains the main pyramid and a smaller, subsidiary pyramid – for the pharaoh's spirit or ka – which has its own enclosing wall. In the space between the two concentric walls there are nine more small pyramids, for the pharaoh's wives. Though these are of different sizes, and not regularly positioned, each has its own enclosure. Two of them share an enclosure, and another two share a 'party wall' between their enclosures. These relationships evident in the enclosures seem to 'say' something about the relationships of the people buried in them. But the most noticeable characteristic of the walls is their geometry. Though never quite square in plan, they are laid out orthogonally, taking the lead from the orientation of the central pyramid, and thereby reinforcing the relationship between the pyramid complex and the passage of the sun through the sky.

Some higher-status Egyptian houses also had walls which enclosed private space around them. This example is from Tel-el-Amarna (c.1400BC). The outermost wall defines the boundary of the possessed ground and space, but the enclosure is also subdivided, around the main house, by subsidiary walls, making spaces for different purposes, and managing movement through the grounds. By these, the main house does not stand detached, but is attached to the boundary wall; and the enclosure becomes a 'patchwork' of contained spaces.

Reference for the house at Tel-al-Amarna:
R.D. Martienssen – *The Idea of Space in Greek Architecture*, 1968, p.8.

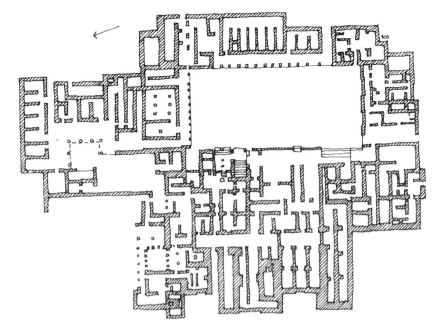

One of the characteristics of the palaces of the ancient Minoan civilisation on the Mediterranean island of Crete is that they appear to have been conceived as built *around rather than within* an orthogonal enclosure, which changes the character of the walls that define the enclosure – they are permeable rather than impregnable. This characteristic is also interpreted as suggesting that defence was not the highest priority for Minoan architects, that their civilisation was based on peaceful cohabitation between palaces rather than struggle and war. It is speculated that the enclosures at the hearts of the Minoan places were used for games (dangerous games) involving wild bulls and athletic youths – as if the forerunners of Spanish bull rings. The drawing shows the plan of the palace of Mallia, which was built sometime around 1400BC.

Reference for Mallia:
James Walter Graham – *The Palaces of Crete*, 1962, fig.6.

Reference for Mycenae:
Carl Schuchhardt – *Schliemann's Discoveries of the Ancient World*, 1979, p.299.

By contrast the architects of the approximately contemporary Mycenaean civilisation on the mainland of Greece were making strongholds fortified with thick defensive walls. Built on rough high ground, these walls could not readily be given ideal geometric form, and follow the irregular topography of the site.

The plan is of the palace of Mycenae. Part of the outer wall has collapsed sometime during the three thousand years or so since it was built, and the full layout of the palace (which was excavated in the nineteenth century by the German archaeologist Heinrich Schliemann) is unclear. The perfectly circular enclosure just inside the famous 'Lion Gate' (at the extreme left of the plan) was a grave pit. You can also see the megaron – the seat of King Agamemnon – near the middle of the enclosure.

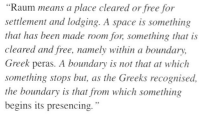

"Raum *means a place cleared or free for settlement and lodging. A space is something that has been made room for, something that is cleared and free, namely within a boundary, Greek* peras. *A boundary is not that at which something stops but, as the Greeks recognised, the boundary is that from which something begins its presencing.*"

Martin Heidegger, translated by Albert Hofstadter – 'Building Dwelling Thinking' (1952), in *Poetry, Language, Thought*, 1975, p.154.

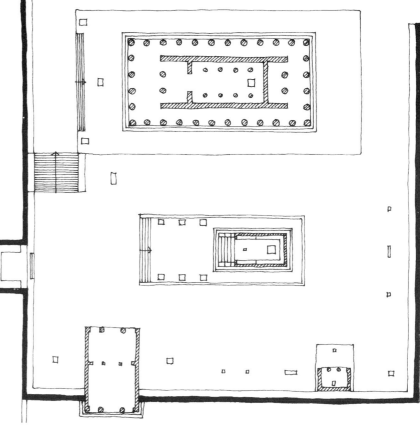

The Greeks created a sacred enclosure – called a temenos – around their temples. The wall of the temenos separated the special domain of the temple from the ordinary world outside. In some cases these had an elegant orthogonal layout, related to the geometry of the temple (above, at Sunion). But more often the temenos of the temple was laid out with a subtle appreciation of the topography of the site (below, the Acropolis in Athens).

Reference for Sunion:
William Taylor – *Greek Architecture*, 1971, p.63.

Reference for the Acropolis in Athens:
Roland Martin – *Living Architecture: Greek*, 1967, p.174.

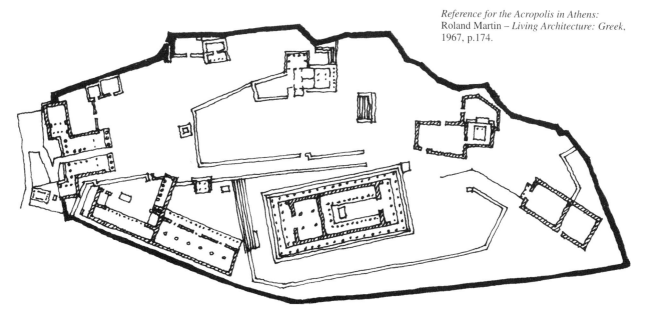

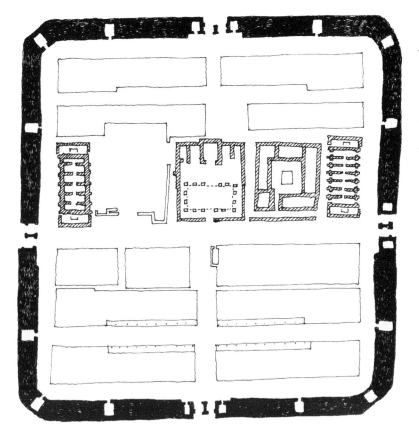

Throughout their empire the Romans built fortresses to a pattern with standard characteristics. The enclosure of defensive walls was rectangular, often square, with gates in the middle of each of the four walls. Except where absolutely unavoidable, the rectangular plan took no account of local topographical conditions; it was imposed by authority. The four gateways set up a cross of roads within, leading to the most important building – the principia – at the centre. In this way, the enclosure walls were not only defensive but set up the order within. They established four cardinal directions (not necessarily those of north, south, east, and west, but four 'Roman' directions in each location) stretching, by their roads, out into the surrounding country. The walls constituted a boundary between the disciplined Roman mind-set, encapsulated in the fort, and the other world outside, there to be conquered and controlled.

The drawing is the plan of Gelligaer, in Wales, at the very north-western edge of the Roman Empire.

Reference for Gelligaer:
Elisabeth Whittle – *A Guide to Ancient and Historic Wales: Glamorgan and Gwent*, 1992, pp.66-8.

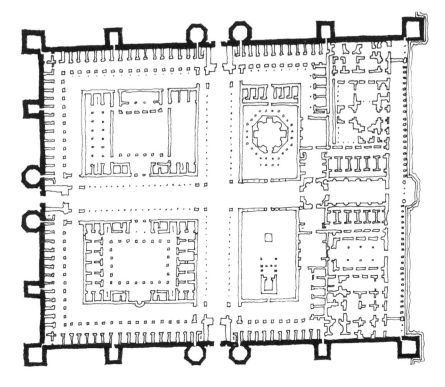

Even when they were not building primarily for defence and control, Roman architects followed similar patterns. The lower drawing is the plan of the palace of the emperor Diocletian, at Spalato on the coast of Dalmatia (now Split in Croatia). One side of the palace (at the right of the drawing) was on the edge of the Adriatic Sea; one imagines that the walls of the enclosure separated the ordinary world from a world of extreme privilege and pleasure.

Reference for the palace of the emperor Diocletian at Split:
Frank E. Brown – *Roman Architecture*, 1964, fig.92.

117

While the architects of Dubrovnik (south from Split along the coast of Croatia) had to build defensive walls around their city (above), their rivals in Venice, at the northern end of the Adriatic, could rely on the natural enclosure of its lagoon. Both enclosures – the walls of Dubrovnik and the lido and lagoon of Venice – though once protecting living cities, now reinforce the separation of major tourist places, with their romantic experiences, from the everyday world.

Reference for Dubrovnik:
Miljenko Foretic – *Dubrovnik*, 1997.

Reference for Venice:
Italo Calvino, translated by William Weaver – *Invisible Cities*, 1972.

"In the Han image (left), the world of man is a clearing marked off from the unknown on all four sides by symbols in animal form.... first the Blue Dragon of the East.... To the south is the Red Phoenix of summer and fire at the zenith. Next there is the west and the White Tiger of the metallic autumn, symbolic of weapons, war, executions, and harvest; of fruitful conclusion and the calmness of twilight, of memory and regret, and unalterable past mistakes. It is the end of the road, but not the end of the cycle, for the new beginning will have to come from the all-inclusive darkness of winter. Its position is the cold region of the north; its color, black, and its element, water. There time is immeasurable and elastic. Pictured here is... a snake coiling around a turtle, two hibernating reptiles forming a picture behind man's back of life preserved underground."

"Facing south, his feet firmly on the fifth element, the earth, is man.... not knowing how high is up, how deep is down, and how far away is the end of the world in each direction – man fixes his position as equidistant from the end of the universe on all sides, and places himself squarely in the middle. He is not represented by any picture, but his desire is expressed clearly in the abstract form of writing. Scattered inside the square world of man are these words: 'One thousand autumns and ten thousand years, enduring happiness, never to end!' Hundreds of designs similar to this one are found on tiles and bricks from Han sites – self-portraits of the houses or cities of which the tiles were a part."

"The rectangular Han dynasty tile... is a rigid, finite, and unnatural design. Wherever circumstances permit, this image is readily translated into the equally unnatural classical city plan of China, sometimes using the same animal symbols to name the gates at corresponding cardinal points. It manifests an intellectual order superimposed upon a natural terrain.... This rationalized basic design is not only frequently seen in city plans but is also sensed in the layout of houses, palaces, and tombs. Always keeping man at its center, it is an image of man's society, organizing its enclosed space around him...."

"... The drama of Chinese architecture's struggle to meet the requirement of its program is thus one of ingenious exploration of the potentialities of the wall, the height of the platform, the placing of individual buildings, the organization of a compound. It concerns itself above all with the prescribed position and movement of man in an architectural complex."

Nelson I. Wu – *Chinese and Indian Architecture*, 1964, pp.11-12, 29-30.

(Left) The 'Forbidden City', Beijing, China

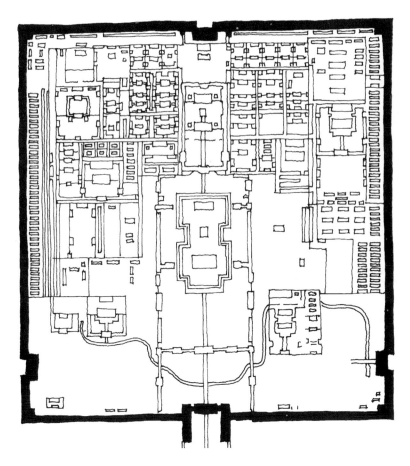

The mosque of al-Azhar in Cairo, built in AD970, is an enclosure of four walls set apart from the everyday world for worship. The orthogonal plan does not relate to the cardinal directions dictated by the sun, but is positioned so that the qibla *wall, at the top in the drawing, with its central symbolic doorway – the* mihrab *– faces Mecca.*

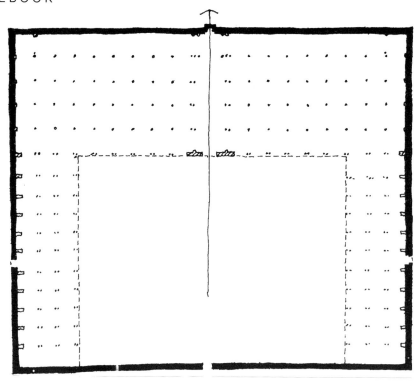

"The mosque is a shelter and a refuge from the turbulent life of the crowded city. Each Friday the thousands its open sahn, *or interior court, and its covered prayer hall accommodate bow down in unison toward the* qibla *wall which faces Mecca. All over the world they turn toward the one center..."*

The Generalife, near the Alhambra in Granada in southern Spain, is a 'paradise garden' composed of many enclosed courtyards, each with its own character. (The long flight of steps at the top right of the drawing is that illustrated on page 24 of Analysing Architecture.*)*

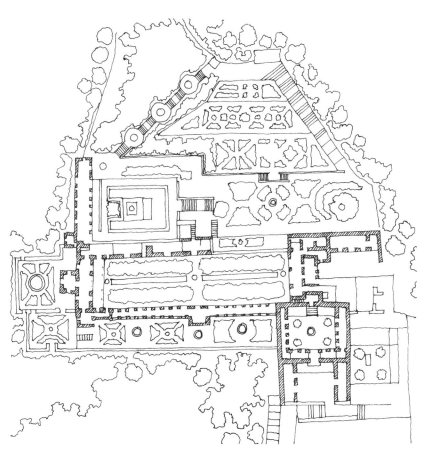

"Throughout the Koran, when Muhammad speaks of paradise, he constantly used the phrase, 'Gardens beneath which rivers flow'.... In the Koran, the word firdaws *is used several times for paradise. It comes from the Persian* faradis, *derived from a word meaning a place walled in, or the finest and highest part of a garden. In the lavish use of fountains, quadripartite courts, and pavilions overlooking basins of water, many Islamic palaces, in their private portions, seem deliberately intended by their builders to provide a setting for the anticipation upon earth of the pleasures of the hereafter."*

John D. Hoag – *Western Islamic Architecture,* 1964, pp.8-9.

120

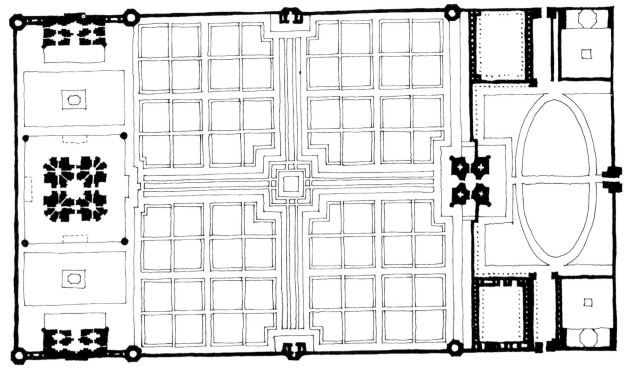

The enclosure of the Taj Mahal, Agra, India, represents a diagram of the structure of heaven.

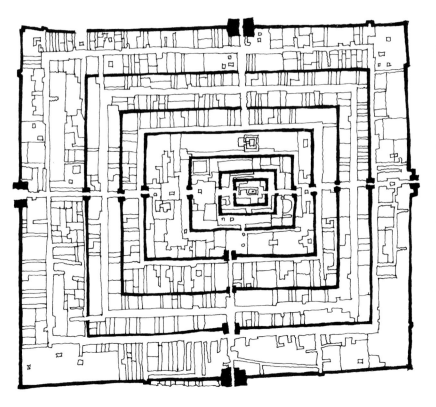

Reference for Taj Mahal:
Christopher Tadgell – *The History of Architecture in India*, 1990, p.255.

"One of the outstanding characteristics of traditional societies is the opposition that they assume between their inhabited territory and the unknown and indeterminate space that surrounds it. The form is the world (more precisely, our world), the cosmos; everything outside it is no longer a cosmos but a sort of 'other world', a foreign, chaotic space, peopled by ghosts, demons, 'foreigners'."

Mircea Eliade, translated by Willard R. Trask – *The Sacred and the Profane: the nature of religion*, 1959, p.29.

"... the holy city of Srirangam [was] built in concentric circles around the temple... a near perfect manifestation of the ancient and mythic vedic notion of the city as a Model of the Cosmos, ... precisely oriented along the four cardinal directions: North, South, East and West."

Kenneth Frampton and Charles Correa – *Charles Correa*, 1996, p.185.

121

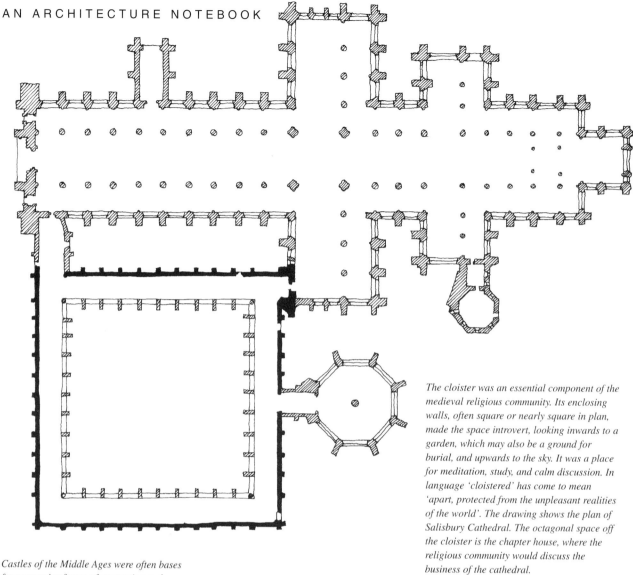

The cloister was an essential component of the medieval religious community. Its enclosing walls, often square or nearly square in plan, made the space introvert, looking inwards to a garden, which may also be a ground for burial, and upwards to the sky. It was a place for meditation, study, and calm discussion. In language 'cloistered' has come to mean 'apart, protected from the unpleasant realities of the world'. The drawing shows the plan of Salisbury Cathedral. The octagonal space off the cloister is the chapter house, where the religious community would discuss the business of the cathedral.

Castles of the Middle Ages were often bases for aggressive forces of oppression and occupation. Their walls, visible symbols of power, were built to provide a safe haven for troops, protected from disruptive attacks by enemies. In sieges those walls could also constitute a prison.

The drawing shows the plan of Conwy Castle, at the mouth of the river Conwy on the coast of north Wales. It was built according to the design of James of St George, for King Edward I of England, during the years 1283-87. When complete its walls were limewashed, increasing their visible expression of power and confidence.

Reference for Conwy Castle:
Arnold Taylor – Conwy Castle and Town Walls, 1998.

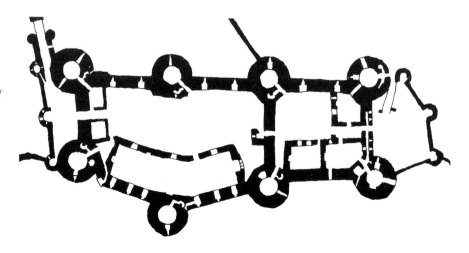

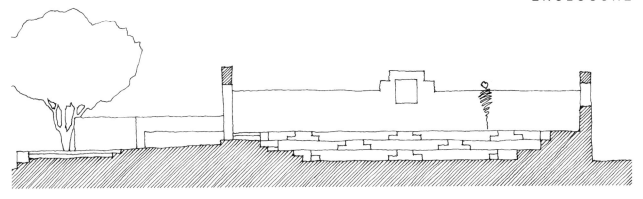

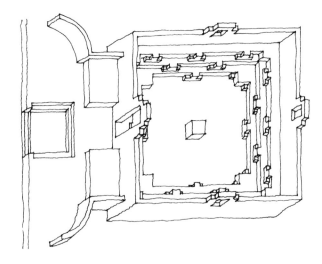

"The traditional kunds, generally located next to temples, are rectangular water ponds where the faithful come for ritual purification before entering the temple to worship.... The Surya Kund, a re-incarnation of these traditional kunds... is a tank where one comes to think.... Like its prototypes, the orientation of the Surya Kund (by Charles Correa) has been precisely determined by the cardinal directions of the compass."

Kenneth Frampton and Charles Correa – *Charles Correa*, 1996, pp.186-7.

*"Can this cockpit hold
The vasty fields of France? or may we cram
Within this wooden O the very casques
That did affright the air at Agincourt?"*

William Shakespeare – *Henry V*, Chorus.

The enclosing wall of the Globe, Shakespeare's theatre rebuilt on the south bank of the river Thames in London, preserves the privacy and seclusion of the performance area. As one approaches the theatre one's sense of excitement and anticipation of the drama is enhanced by the separation of the place from everywhere else. When one is inside, the wall also acts like a 'lens' to focus attention on the make-believe action on stage.

Reference for the Globe theatre:
J.R. Mulryne and Margaret Shewring (editors) – *Shakespeare's Globe Rebuilt*, 1997.

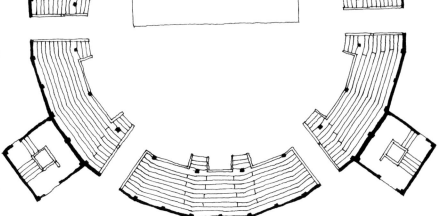

The wall around the Ryoanji Temple Garden, near Kyoto, in Japan, frames large natural boulders set in raked grit, like islands in the sea. The wall mediates between the precise domain of this work of art and the world outside, helping to make it a place for contemplation.

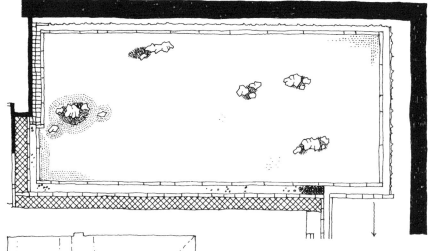

The wall around Mies van der Rohe's design for a 'Three Courtyard House' (1934) frames the domain of the house. The closedness of the wall contrasts with the openness of the house, only the 'T'-shaped portion of which is roofed. It sets the precise limits of the house's 'world'. It also establishes the underlying geometry of the structure and the spatial organisation of the house.

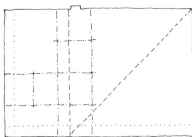

Reference for Ryoanji Temple Garden:
William Alex – *Japanese Architecture*, 1965, figs.116-18.

Reference for Mies van der Rohe's 'Three Courtyard House':
Philip Johnson – *Mies van der Rohe*, 1978, pp.102-3.

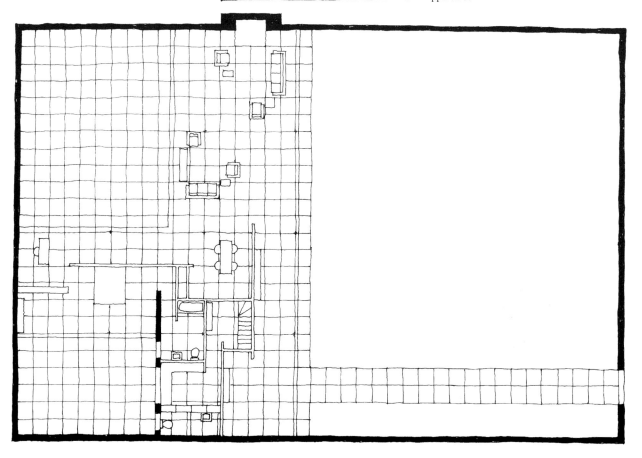

Many houses, in many countries, in many periods of history have been designed from an enclosing wall inwards, rather than as objects in space. The private space of the house is delimited and defined by the perimeter wall, and then that space is divided into various rooms and courtyards. Often the division of space was according to standard patterns belonging to particular cultures. Below is an ancient Greek house on the island of Delos.

On the right is a plan of part of the ancient Greek city of Olynthus, composed of five blocks each of ten houses. Looking at such plans one realises the obvious fact that the density of all cities depends on the invention of the wall. Its role as support for shelter is secondary to the way it allows many of the activities of domestic life to happen much closer together than would otherwise be possible.

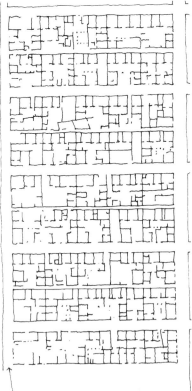

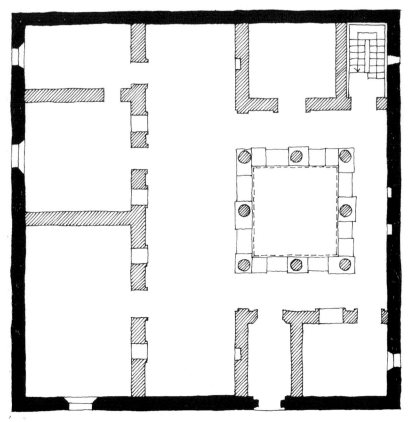

Sometimes the sites of ancient Greek urban houses were not regular. Still they 'began' conceptually with the perimeter enclosing wall. This is another house from Delos (drawn at a different scale).

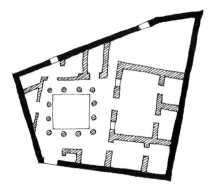

Reference for Greek houses on Delos:
R.D. Martienssen – *The Idea of Space in Greek Architecture*, 1968, p.53.

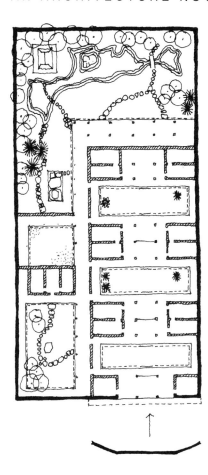

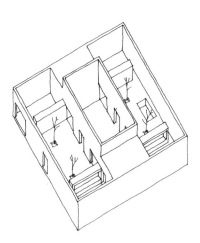

The Casa Gaspar, by Alberto Campo Baeza, is not a city house. It stands in an orange grove near Cadiz in Spain. Its enclosing walls provide privacy in the landscape. They also make the house introverted, with distant views only upwards, to the sky. All the walls of the house are white, reflecting light in different ways.

Reference for Casa Gaspar:
John Welsh – Modern House, 1995, pp.56-63.

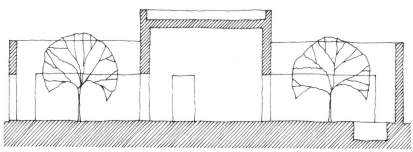

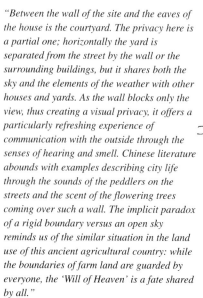

"Between the wall of the site and the eaves of the house is the courtyard. The privacy here is a partial one; horizontally the yard is separated from the street by the wall or the surrounding buildings, but it shares both the sky and the elements of the weather with other houses and yards. As the wall blocks only the view, thus creating a visual privacy, it offers a particularly refreshing experience of communication with the outside through the senses of hearing and smell. Chinese literature abounds with examples describing city life through the sounds of the peddlers on the streets and the scent of the flowering trees coming over such a wall. The implicit paradox of a rigid boundary versus an open sky reminds us of the similar situation in the land use of this ancient agricultural country: while the boundaries of farm land are guarded by everyone, the 'Will of Heaven' is a fate shared by all."

Nelson I. Wu – Chinese and Indian Architecture, 1964, p.32.

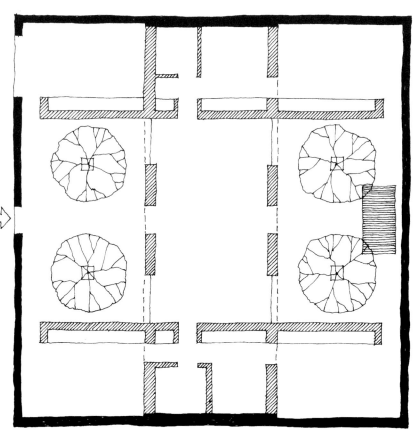

LABYRINTH AND DATUM

LABYRINTH AND DATUM

"Now, before Daedalus left Crete, he had given Ariadne a magic ball of thread, and instructed her how to enter and leave the Labyrinth. She must open the entrance door and tie the loose end of the thread to the lintel; the ball would then roll along, diminishing as it went and making, with devious turns and twists, for the innermost recess where the Minotaur was lodged. This ball Ariadne gave to Theseus, and instructed him to follow it until he reached the sleeping monster, whom he must seize by the hair and sacrifice to Poseidon. He could then find his way back by rolling up the thread into a ball again."

Robert Graves – *The Greek Myths*, 1955, no.98.

"The way that can be known is not the way."

Lao Tzu – *Tao Te Ching*.

"Death in Venice was a response to all the evils in the world. I lived behind it. I was blocked – walled in."

Susan Kaiser Vogel, quoted in Jan Butterfield (editor) – *The Art of Light and Space*, 1993, p.208.

Walls are used to enclose space, and to demarcate areas of ground surface. They are also used to channel pathways, to modify entrances and exits, to manipulate routes and serial experiences, all of which take time. There is a relationship between walls and the inescapability, and experience, of time and space. Walls are an instrument of control over both.

In these relationships, walls are not things to be looked at (though they are seen); their purpose is to differentiate between accessible space and matter which is inaccessible. The operative element is the surface. And the inaccessible realm is indeterminate, even conceptually infinite.

In 1978 Susan Kaiser Vogel walled herself into her studio in Venice, California. She called the work *Death in Venice*. As the name of the piece implies, the wall itself can be interpreted as a symbol of death. But it also made a 'tomb' for the living artist, a place in which, physically at least, she incontrovertibly 'knew' exactly where she was, and had no options for movement in any direction. Though in-

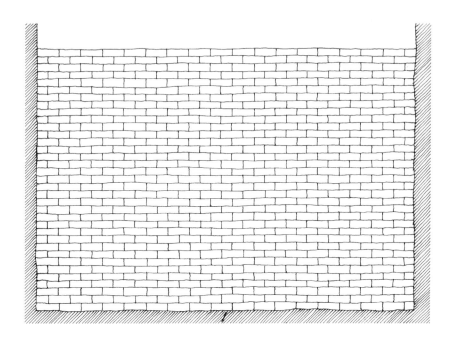

tellectually the work may be a labyrinth, the denial of movement dictated by the wall makes the space she inhabited the antithesis of a labyrinth, minus even the choice of exit and entrance.

James Turrell also works with space and light. He uses walls in various ways. In 1989 he began work on the Irish Sky Garden in south-west Ireland, near Skibereen. The entrance to the garden is through an opening in a stone wall. The doorway is in the form of a simple trilithon – two posts and a lintel. It marks the beginning of a route through a contrived landscape, along which one is manipulated in various ways, particularly in how one looks at the sky. (A plan of the garden is on the opposite page. 'The Mound', 'The Pyramid', and 'The Grotto' are illustrated on page 62, in the chapter on the 'Artificial Cave'.)

"...from now on there are no more tracks and paths, only an interplay of viewpoints to guide the walker in his progress. And if, as he wanders around the Sky Garden, he should look back again at the point where he entered, all he will see framed in the narrow portal is the airy brightness of the Irish sky, in all its limitless promise."

Oliver Wick – *James Turrell: Irish Sky Garden*, 1992, p.29.

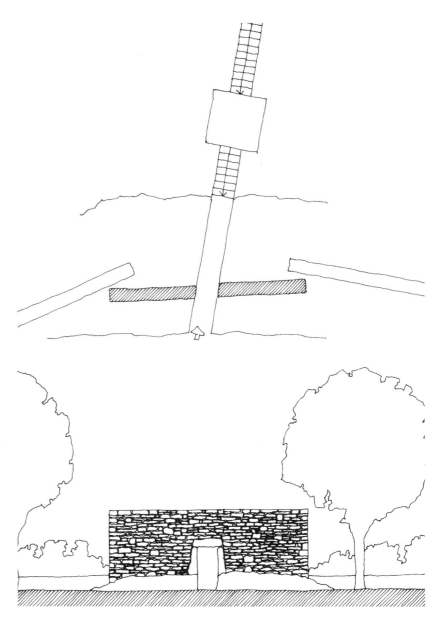

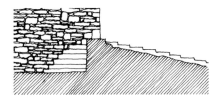 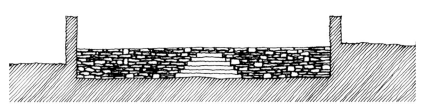

"Once the viewer leaves the Mound, he has already changed direction, following the shift in the natural lie of the land from a right-angled alignment of the lake to a parallel one.... The right hand wall of the [Mound's exit] corridor continues outside as a high wall leading across the hump-backed moraine to the Sky Wall at right angles to it. Its upper edge forms a straight horizontal line across the viewer's field of vision, while the foot of the wall accommodates the irregularities of the topography. In this way, the naturally restricted panoramic view is blocked. The wall cuts into the Irish Sky like a new horizon.... Halfway along, on the left edge of the wood, another wall begins. Thus the viewer find his walk ending in a yard-like enclosure in front of the obstruction of the Sky Wall, which prevents him both from seeing and from advancing further. At its centre, a set of steps, three-sided and narrowing towards the top, leads up to the crest of the wall. Having seen nothing but sky before climbing them, the viewer now finds the gently undulating landscape of West Cork spread out before his gaze. On the far horizon, the peak of Carrig Fada recalls once more the spiritual association between the Sky Garden and the prehistoric cultures of Ireland."

Oliver Wick – *James Turrell: Irish Sky Garden*, 1992, p.35.

The opening in the wall stimulates a sense of anticipation, an opportunity to move into a series of experiences. The wall determines a beginning.

Turrell uses a similar stone wall in a very different way within the garden. 'The Sky Wall' (above) blocks one's way after one has emerged from 'The Mound'. Instead of offering a 'beginning' it seems, at first, to present an 'end' – a horizon cutting across the sky. Here the 'way' forward is to climb the steps, revealing the landscape beyond.

In these instances walls affect experience. They influence movement, offer beginnings, obstacles... and ends. They suggest, or determine, direction.

In a plan a wall is a line drawn on surface of a piece of paper. In reality a wall is a line drawn on the surface of the ground. The boundaries a wall suggests on paper become real on the ground. Architects use

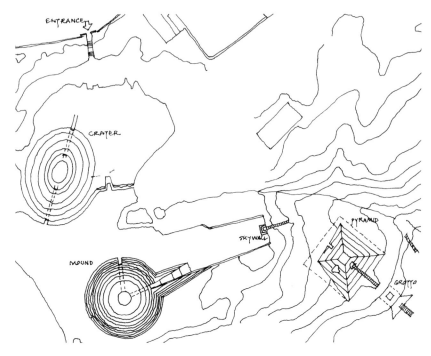

walls to demarcate space. They also use them to manage movement, in simple and in complex ways, sometimes clarifying routes, sometimes confusing them.

Often, such manipulation of movement by means of a wall occurs at an entrance or exit to a space.

The Cemetery Chapel at Kemi in Finland (right), designed by Osmo Sipari and built in 1960, is a building in which walls are used to identify places. The main place of the chapel, together with its subsidiary rooms, is identified by a pair of parallel walls, which also support the chapel's roof. There are two other significant walls in the plan. The first of these, at right-angles to the pair of parallel walls, leads from the entrance through the cemetery to the door of the chapel, clearly defining the approach. The second, parallel to the principal walls, penetrates the space of the chapel, indicating an exit. Together the two walls define the area of the garden.

The intention at Kemi seems to have been to make entrance to the chapel clear and direct. Architects responsible for places of defence have often had an opposite intention. The gateways of the Golconda Citadel in India (right) are protected by walls that make entrance tortuous rather than direct, slowing down attackers.

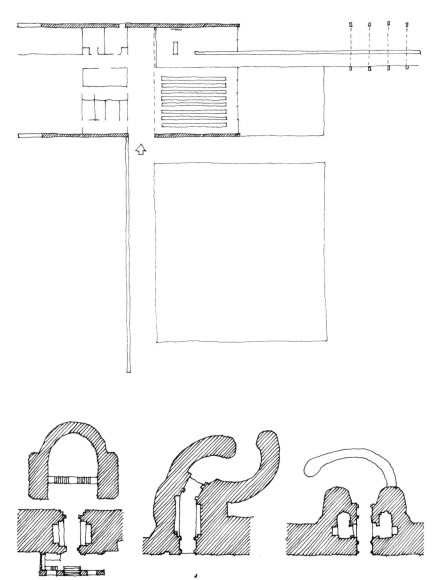

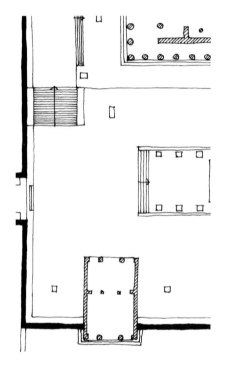

Entrance to the temenos of a temple in ancient Greece was usually modified by a pair of parallel walls with a roof over them, called a propylon (left). The walls had the effect of stretching the transition between the outside and the inside of the sacred precinct, enhancing the separation of the temple from the everyday world. The walls also seem sometimes to have been positioned to present a particular view of the temple as one enters the temenos.

At a more domestic scale, walls related to entrances have been used to modify the way in which even quite small spaces are used and experienced.

The internal partition walls of this small house (below) at Barnhouse on Orkney off the north coast of Scotland are formed of slabs of stone standing upright. They are not load bearing, but, like the partitions in a Le Corbusian 'dom-ino' space,

act independently to organise space into places for use, and (in this instance) perhaps for possession by different family individuals. Here their main purpose is to give privacy and protection from draughts to the bedchambers embedded in the thick outer walls. There is one other partition wall, leading in from the entrance, which divides the main space of the house into two rooms. This wall, with its adjacent opening positioned as far from the doorway as possible, lengthens the journey from the entrance into this room, increasing its privacy and protection from draughts.

Something similar happens in the plan below. This is a slate-workers' cottage from north Wales. The wall to the side of the entrance lengthens the transition from outside to inside, helps with draught protection, and makes a small sitting place by the fire.

In this ancient Egyptian mortuary temple, attached to the base of a pyramid at Meidum, walls were positioned to prevent a direct view of the altar from outside.

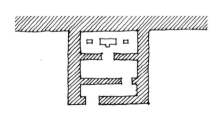

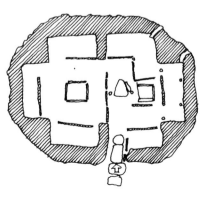

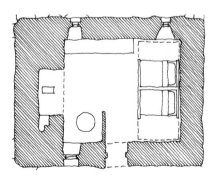

Tadao Ando's design for the Church of the Light, in Osaka (below), uses a simple rectangular cell to make the main space of the chapel. Around this he wrapped a separate wall which partly obscures the cell of the chapel, but also penetrates it, making the entrance and a lobby space.

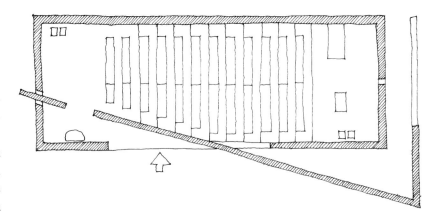

Walls have been used to modify entrance in more recent works of architecture too.

In Tadao Ando's plan for the Church of the Light, at Osaka in Japan (top right, 1987-89), a wall strikes diagonally across the orthogonal chapel. The wall makes a small triangular lobby. It also modifies people's experience of entering the chapel, introducing at least two additional changes of direction, and 'delivering' them into the main chamber nearer its central axis.

As part of his work on the Castelvecchio in Verona in the 1960s, Carlo Scarpa introduced a wall dividing the main entrance (below). The wall makes the entrance more sculptural; it also divides an 'in' route from an 'out'.

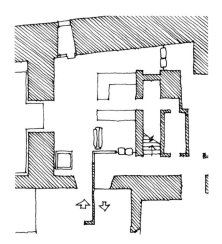

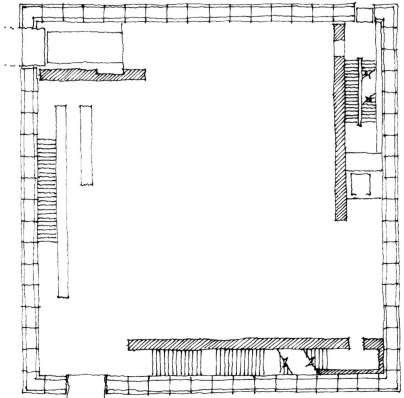

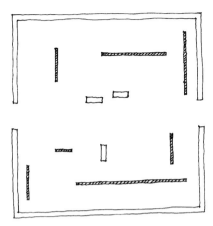

Marcel Breuer's design for a war memorial in Cambridge, Massachusetts, combines death and the idea of the labyrinth.

"To have been located in the path of pedestrians crossing the Cambridge Commons. A square 'island' paved with flagstone and surrounded by low stone benches. Composition of rough plate glass screens cantilevered up from below-grade anchorage. Names of 16,000 Cambridge servicemen and women were to have been baked into the 1" thick, unbreakable, translucent glass slabs."

Reference for Breuer's war memorial:
Peter Blake (editor) – *Marcel Breuer: Sun and Shadow, the philosophy of an architect,* undated.

Reference for Tadao Ando's Church of the Light:
Masao Furuyama – *Tadao Ando,* 1993, p.140.

Reference for Carlo Scarpa's work at the Castelvecchio:
Richard Murphy – *Carlo Scarpa and Castelvecchio,* 1990.

Reference for Peter Zumthor's art gallery at Lake Constance:
Architecture Today, 83, November 1997, p.12.

And, in the art gallery he designed at Lake Constance in southern Germany, Peter Zumthor used walls to modify the way the space of each floor is entered (opposite). The walls define and enclose the spaces occupied by the stairs and the lift. They also dictate that one enters the spaces always along, rather than at right-angles to, the outer glass walls of the gallery.

In many art galleries walls provide the surfaces on which paintings are hung, echoing the way walls accommodated painting in prehistoric times. The walls of art galleries also manage the routes visitors take, and the order in which they see the works exhibited.

In his layout design for an exhibition of his own work, held in the Basilica in Verona in 1998 (below), Sverre Fehn divided the space available with a long diagonal wall, which turned around into small triangular cells at each end. The cells made dark spaces in which video films of Fehn's work were shown, but generally the diagonal wall was not used for display; Fehn's drawings were supported on screens hung from the roof structure of the room, and his models displayed on low plinths. The purpose of the wall was primarily to divide the room and to set up an anticlockwise route around the exhibition, making the space a little more into a labyrinth.

Eduardo Souta de Moura used a similar device when he designed a small art gallery in Porto in the early 1990s. The room of the Clerigos Art Gallery is

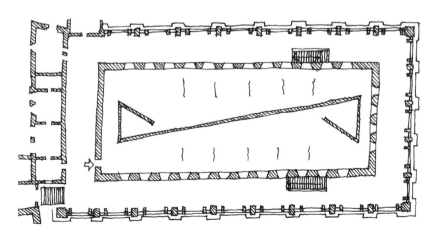

organised into three spaces, and a sequential route created, by the insertion of a diagonal wall with a short 'spur' attached to one of its sides (below). This wall is used for displaying works of art... but some artists have made walls and what they do the subject of their art.

In 1977 Susan Kaiser Vogel built a brick wall at the Frederick S. Wight Art Gallery, in the University of California, Los Angeles. The brick wall wrapped around itself into the simplest form of maze... enclosing a small space, separating it from the world outside, except for a view of the sky. The work was called *Blue Flame*.

Reference for Blue Flame*:*
Jan Butterfield (editor) – *The Art of Light and Space*, 1993, p.207.

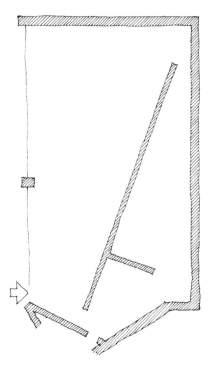

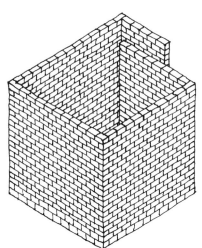

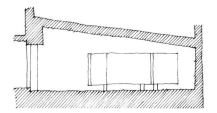

In the Galerie Jean-François Dumont in Bordeaux, Laurent Pariente built an L-shaped wall (right, 1990). The wall itself, and the effect it had on the experience of the space, was the exhibit.

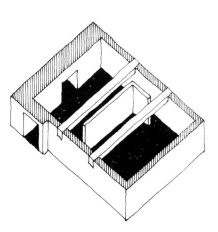

136

"At a certain point we found ourselves again in the original heptagonal room (easily identified because the stairwell began there), and we resumed moving toward our right, trying to go straight from room to room. We went through three rooms and then found ourselves facing a blank wall. The only opening led into a new room that had only one other aperture, which we went through, and then, after another four rooms, we found ourselves again facing a wall. We returned to the previous room, which had two exits, took the one we had not tried before, went into a new room, and then found ourselves back in the heptagonal room of the outset."

Umberto Eco – *The Name of the Rose*, 1983, p.171.

And in 1996 Pariente constructed a much more complex labyrinth in the galleries of the Henry Moore Institute in Leeds (below). The work engaged the visitor with the unnerving uncertainty of being lost in a maze, but also provided a rich variety of effects of light and shade, and views from one space into another.

of enclosure, prevent an overview of the layout of the pathway, and dramatically increase the sense of concern at becoming lost.

A maze identifies a place of uncertainty. It works by directly engaging anyone who experiences it in making decisions which might or might not have positive

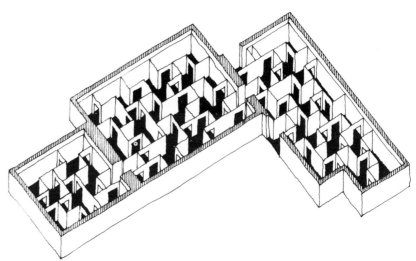

Labyrinths and mazes have fascinated human minds for thousands of years. Though their principal element is a line of passage, a pathway which might only be marked out as a line on a pavement, their effect is greatly increased if that pathway is determined by a layout of walls higher than eye-level. The walls increase the sense

results in terms of finding one's way either to the centre or to the exit. In this the maze has been considered a metaphor of life, of the chances and decisions involved in finding a pathway through existence.

Some labyrinths are found inscribed in the floors or walls of temples and churches, presumably as indication that the

Reference for Laurent Pariente:
Robert Hooper – *Laurent Pariente*, 1996.

relevant god holds a master plan that may not be read directly by mortals caught in the maze itself.

Mazes might be as simple as this spiral pavement maze at Thornton in Leicestershire (right), or they might be as dauntingly complex as that at Hatfield House (below) or the labyrinth at Cawdor Castle (far right).

Mazes such as these have 'solutions' related to finding the appropriate paths... first to reach the 'centre', and then to escape, returning from the mystical to the ordinary world. A labyrinth has a single route to solution which, though it may be

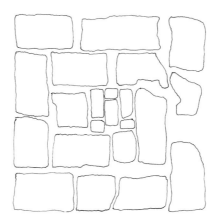

very tortuous, does not involve choice. A maze is different in that it incorporates junctions where choices must be made, and

The graffiti on a wall in Pompeii illustrates a labyrinth. The inscription reads, "Labyrinth here lives the Minotaur".

From Nigel Pennick – *Mazes and Labyrinths,* 1990, p.15.

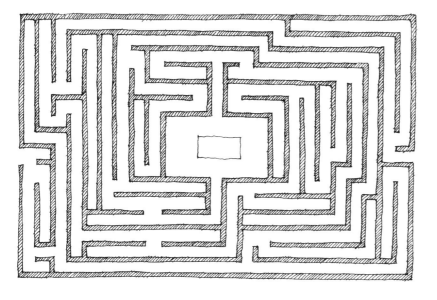

"Without being over-hasty in deciding the original meaning and function of labyrinths, there is no doubt that they included the notion of defending a 'centre'. Not everyone might try to enter a labyrinth or return unharmed from one; to enter it was equivalent to an initiation. The 'centre' might be one of a variety of things. The labyrinth could be defending a city, a tomb or a sanctuary but, in every case, it was defending some magico-religious space that must be made safe from the uncalled, the uninitiated."

Mircea Eliade, translated by Rosemary Sheed – *Patterns in Comparative Religion,* 1958, p.381.

138

"Some run the Shepherd's Race – a rut
Within a grass-plot deeply cut
And wide enough to tread –
A maze of path, of old designed
To tire the feet, perplex the mind,
Yet pleasure heart and head;
'Tis not unlike this life we spend,
And where you start from, there you end."

Bradfield – *Sentan's Wells*, 1864, quoted in
Nigel Pennick – *Mazes and Labyrinths*, 1990,
p.13.

Le Corbusier based a number of designs for
museums and art galleries on the idea of a
labyrinth. Some, he intended, could be
endlessly expandable.

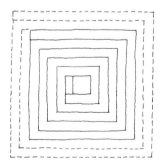

dead ends which cause consternation and frustration. The only uncertainty in a labyrinth is that of not knowing when one will reach the centre, and then not knowing exactly when one will find one's way out. The uncertainties in a maze are much greater, and there lingers at the back of one's mind the thought that one might never find the centre, nor escape.

Architects, of course, like 'gods', 'hold' the master-plans of the buildings they design. All works of architecture involving the organisation of many spaces may be considered, to some degree, as

mazes or labyrinths. Simple combinations of a few spaces can provide serial experiences, but do not provoke the confusion and frustrations associated with, and cultivated by, recreational or spiritual mazes.

This small tomb enclosure, for the Pini family in Parabiagio (right), designed by Gabriele Mucchi in the late 1940s, consists of an enclosing wall with an entrance, a pathway which leads to some steps up to a smaller enclosure (with the tombs) which is the 'goal' or centre of this simple maze. There is no opportunity to get lost in this uncomplicated layout.

When works of architecture involve the composition of many spaces, with different sizes and relationships, the possibility of their becoming more like mazes or labyrinths becomes much greater. The plan below shows the layout (as restored by R.N. Kennedy) of the Women's Baths in the ruins of the ancient Roman villa of Hadrian at Tivoli near Rome. If one imagines oneself in the spaces of the plan, this would have been a building in which it was easy to lose one's 'bearings', a maze of hot dry rooms and steam rooms, cold baths and hot baths....

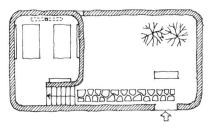

"On a wide comparison, important tombs are generally labyrinthine..."

William Richard Lethaby – *Architecture, Mysticism and Myth*, 1892, p.172.

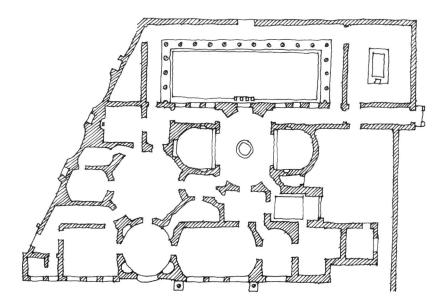

The Women's Baths at Tivoli must have been something of a maze. Rooms pass one to the next without reference to a datum space. The disorientation would have been increased by the passageways between rooms being sometimes diagonal, at the corners, and by the rarity of simple rectangular spaces. Maybe the sense of gentle disorientation in a building devoted to pleasure was intentional.

Reference for R.N. Kennedy's restoration of the Women's Baths at Hadrian's Villa:
John F. Harbeson – *The Study of Architectural Design*, 1927, p.217.

Reference for the Pini tomb:
G.E. Kidder-Smith – *Italy Builds*, 1954, p.182.

John Soane's plan of the Bank of England (below) was consciously reminiscent of the plans of ancient Roman buildings. The shapes of the grand spaces it contained were not always dictated by walls of uniform thickness, but fitted together rather like a badly made jigsaw, with the walls as 'joints' between the pieces. It must have been difficult to maintain one's orientation, and sense of direction, within the bank, and have taken occupants some time to attain a mental map of the relationships between the variety of rooms, halls, and outside courtyards.

Finding one's way through the old Bank of England (right), with its patchwork of courtyards, banking halls, and offices, must have been like finding one's way through a maze. This plan was designed by John Soane, and realised between 1788 and 1826.

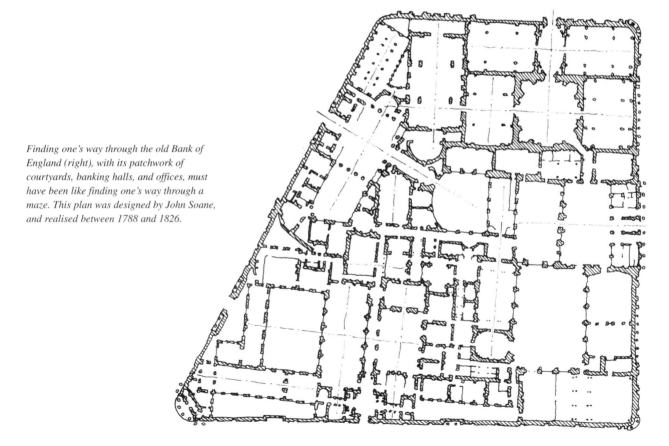

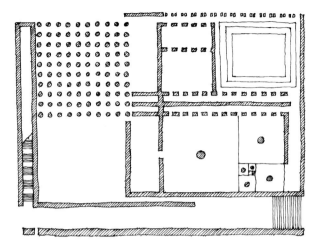

In the Divine Comedy *Dante described the descent through the seven levels of hell as being like Theseus's journey through the Cretan labyrinth of the Minotaur. When Giuseppe Terragni designed a memorial to Dante – Il Danteum – which was intended to be built in Rome, he made it an enigmatic labyrinth, not just in plan, but in the vertical dimension too.*

Some architects have made the plans of their buildings like mazes intentionally.

Luis Barragán designed a house for himself in the 1940s. It was built in Mexico City. His intention seems to have been to avoid creating a simple, easily legible layout of rooms. The sequence from entrance to the space that might be considered the heart of the house is managed by walls of different types and in a variety of relationships with one another. Barragán's aim was apparently to make the deep interior of the living spaces seem further away from the ordinary world of the street outside (more secluded, more 'monastic' perhaps) than they actually were. The route of this maze takes one from the main entrance to the stair hall, which has no view of the outside, and which is lit mysteriously from above. At that point one changes direction, turning right towards the living room. Here the entrance is 'blocked' by a wall that does not go to the ceiling, making one turn left and see the window onto the garden. The

Reference for Barragán's house in Mexico City:
Raúl Rispa (editor) – *Barragán, the complete works*, 1996.

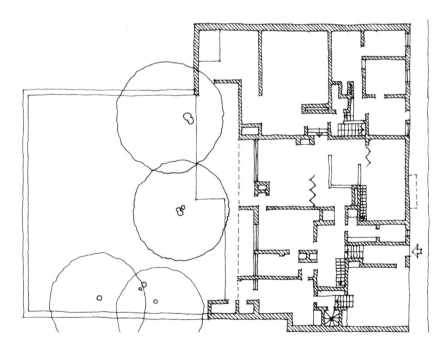

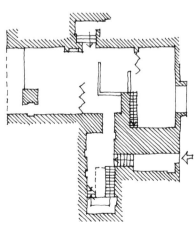

A piece of music can be like a labyrinth, or even a set of labyrinths superimposed on each other. Its order, in conventional music, is maintained by the key, the stave, the bar lines... all of which help musicians know where in the piece they are, and to coordinate their parts with others.

house, as an instrument of change, has 'transported' one from the dust of the street to the luxuriant green 'paradise' of the garden. And the prime instruments of that change are the walls, and their disposition to define a maze-like sequence of spaces.

A piece of music is like a labyrinth. It has a beginning and an end, separated by time. Between the two are lines of melody, incidents of harmony, nuances of rhythm, subtleties of dynamic. A labyrinth can be like a piece of music. An architect can manipulate the different experiences of a combination of spaces, orchestrating light, acoustic, pace... and many other things to create a sequence of effects. The nineteenth-century German Friedrich von Schelling said that "architecture in general

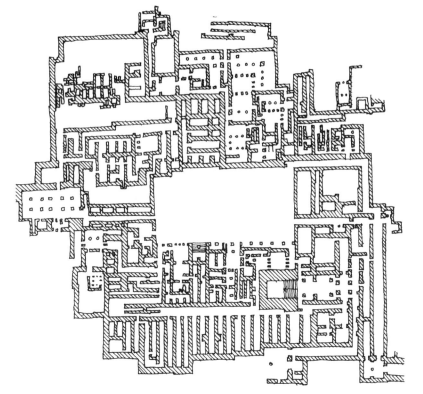

The palace of Minos at Knossos on the island of Crete is traditionally associated with the legend of Theseus and the Minotaur (see the quotation on page 129). Whether it was or was not the labyrinth in the legend, its vast and complex range of rooms on different levels must have made it seem like a mysterious maze in which a stranger could easily get lost.

Reference for the Palace of Minos at Knossos: J.D.S. Pendlebury – A Handbook to the Palace of Minos at Knossos, 1935.

143

is frozen music". In the sense that it can incorporate movement and change, the 'music' of architecture need not be thought of as 'frozen'.

Just as musicians need a framework on which music is written, to help them know where they are (in both pitch and tempo), so too people who use large and complex buildings can benefit from some datum by which they can place themselves and find their ways. Some architects might make their buildings into mazes for conscious effect – to manipulate the ways, and sequences, in which they are experienced. But if a building is unintelligible in ways that cause consternation rather than entertainment....

Architects have used various ways to enable people to understand the layout of large buildings. They have used the orthogonal layout of buildings to establish 'centres', and the 'six directions' (forward, back, left, right, up, down... north, south, east, west... see the chapter 'Geometry in Architecture', *Analysing Architecture*, pp. 99-128) which seem to 'make sense of' the otherwise infinite multitude of possible directions apparent on the surface of the earth.

Even in his 'maze-like' buildings – the Brick House of 1922 and the Barce-

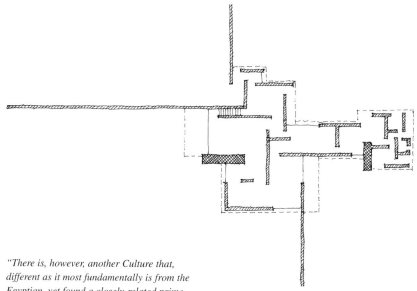

"There is, however, another Culture that, different as it most fundamentally is from the Egyptian, yet found a closely-related prime symbol. This is the Chinese, with its intensely directional principle of the Tao. But whereas the Egyptian treads to the end a way that is prescribed for him with an inexorable necessity, the Chinaman wanders through his world..."

Oswald Spengler, translated by Atkinson – *The Decline of the West*, Volume 1, 1918, p.190

Mies van der Rohe designed his project for a Brick House in the early 1920s. It proposes the idea of the house, not as a neat segmentation into separate rooms, but as relaxed 'maze' – spaces 'flowing' one to the next, separated one from others, but not enclosed. The Barcelona Pavilion, 1929, was a development of this idea. In both Mies maintained the authority of orthogonality.

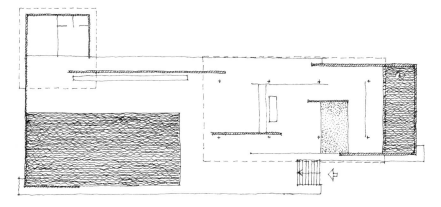

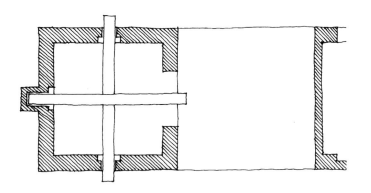

Reference for the Chapel of the Great Cross: Friedrich Achleitner (introduction) – *Walter Pichler: drawings, sculpture, buildings,* 1994, p.93.

lona Pavilion of 1929 – Mies van der Rohe allowed orthogonality to prevail in the arrangement of the walls, so a sense of direction is never completely confused.

In his design for the Beyeler Art Museum in Basel, Switzerland (1997, below), Renzo Piano created a maze-like sequence of rooms within the discipline (the musical 'stave') of five parallel walls. These establish the primacy of the four principal horizontal directions, and the openings at each end of the museum help wandering visitors keep some idea of where they are within the building.

enclosed within a cell of walls. The Chapel for the Great Cross (above) is just a few metres square. It was designed in the late 1970s. Pichler used his walls and their arrangement in powerful ways: first, to enclose a space to protect the cross and provide a private space to be in its presence; second, to reinforce the essential orthogonality of the cross with a square plan; and third, to mediate between the cross and the world outside the chapel – the 'head' is protected in its own little apse, the 'arms' reach through the walls to the world outside, and the 'feet' present them-

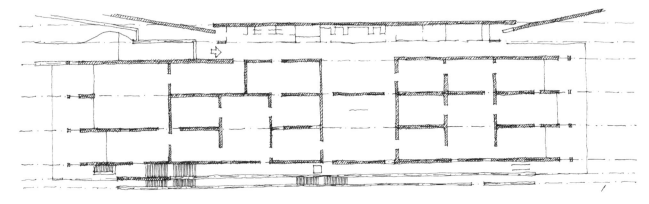

Reference for Renzo Piano's Beyeler Art Museum: *Architectural Review,* December 1997, p.60.

Some architects have used arrangements of walls to establish directions and a centre more strongly.

Walter Pichler has produced a few designs based on a cross lying horizontal,

selves for metaphorical 'kissing' at the door.

The four simple walls are the machinery of this poetry, and establish the cross as a centre.

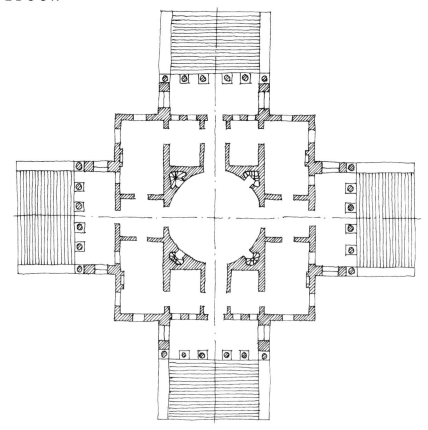

Pichler's arrangement is reminiscent of many cruciform churches, and of Palladio's Villa Rotonda outside Vicenza, where the geometric arrangement of the walls establishes a centre that relates to four principal horizontal directions, as well as to the up and the down. Here the cross is spatial, rather than material, allowing occupation by a human being.

And the spatial definition of a centre plus the six directions is achieved in perhaps the simplest and most direct of ways in this work by Bruce Nauman, titled appropriately Centre of the Universe, and built in 1988. The three square concrete 'tubes' which cross at right angles are large enough for a person to enter. A grill covers the 'down' part that descends into the earth, so that one can stand on the axes

with one's head at the geometric centre, the sky above, the earth below, and the four horizontal directions all around.

Works such as Pichler's Chapel for the Great Cross, Palladio's Villa Rotonda, and Nauman's Centre of the Universe establish a reference point in what they imply is the 'labyrinth' of the world around, just as those who have built temples and

The walls of Palladio's Villa Rotonda (above) and Bruce Nauman's Centre of the Universe (below) establish the six directions and a centre. In doing this they create a datum, a point of reference, within the 'labyrinth' of the world around.

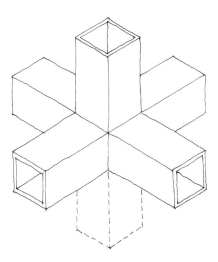

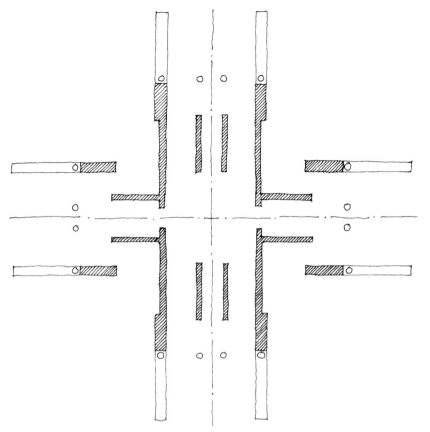

"Solemnly he came forward and mounted the round gunrest. He faced about and blessed gravely thrice the tower, the surrounding country and the awaking mountains."

James Joyce – *Ulysses*, 1922, p.1.

"According to the traditions of an Arunta tribe, the Achilpa, in mythical times the divine being Numbakula cosmicized their future territory, creating their Ancestor, and established their institutions. From the trunk of a gum tree Numbakula fashioned the sacred pole (kauwa-auwa) and, after anointing it with blood, climbed it and disappeared into the sky. This pole represents a cosmic axis, for it is around the sacred pole that territory becomes habitable, hence is transformed into a world."

Mircea Eliade, translated by Willard R. Trask – *The Sacred and the Profane*, 1957, pp.32-3.

Reference for Bruce Nauman's Centre of the Universe:
Jan Butterfield (editor) – *The Art of Light and Space*, 1993, p.150.

churches through history have sought to do. But a building, a garden, a city can be a 'world' within itself.

Probably one of the most important things a mind does in giving intellectual structure to something is to establish a datum, a reference point, an organisational structure. This is the antidote to the maze and labyrinth. In music, traditionally, there are many such datums – the scale of notes, keys, stable beat, the staves and bar structure of written music, accepted musical structures (such as 'sonata form').... In a novel a writer might establish the datum of a character (the narrator or hero of the story) or a place (a city, a monastery, a castle, a house, a secret garden, Sherwood Forest...) or a period of history (the French Revolution, medieval Scotland, ancient Crete...). In writing an academic thesis the datum is the question that is to be answered.

And so on. Such 'points of reference' help communication, build bridges between the creative mind and the mind that 'receives' the work, reassures both that they are focused on the same thing. If the creative mind does not establish the references it may be out of neglect, or an intention to confuse the mind that receives.

Some of the ways in which architects can establish reference points or datums were mentioned in *Analysing Architecture*. A marker (a standing stone, a church steeple...) or a pathway (a road, river, bridge...) might be a datum. A structural grid can establish the intellectual as well as the physical structure of a building. And as has been seen in the work of Pichler, Palladio, and of Nauman, walls can establish a centre and a centrifugal or centripetal set of cardinal axes.

The wall, as one of the most powerful instruments available to the mind of an architect, can help establish datums in these and in other ways too.

In the first decade of the twentieth century Clough Williams-Ellis acquired the house Plas Brondanw in north Wales. He lived there until his death in 1978. During some seventy years he worked on its gardens, imposing ideas, exploiting opportunities, refining subtleties... using it as a laboratory to explore and test ideas. The drawing below is traced from Williams-Ellis's own drawing of the state of the garden by the early 1950s. It has developed into a patchwork of small room-like spaces, defined by quite tall hedges, and larger lawns. The garden is one to explore, moving from 'room' to 'room', each with its different individual character. In such a composition, if thought had not been given to reference points and datums, it might be easy to lose an understanding of exactly where you are. Sometimes, walking around the garden at Plas Brondanw you think you might just be about to get lost. But the ar-

chitect's grip on the larger composition ensures this never quite happens. The house, as the centre of the garden, is the primary datum, but occasionally you lose sight of it. The large sloping lawn in front of the house is also a place where you certainly know where you are. But Williams-Ellis also uses axes, defined partly by the hedge walls, as well as pathways, gateways and ornamental statues, to establish lines and points of reference. One of the most impressive (marked on the plan), which you encounter at various points in an exploration of the garden, makes an alignment with a distant conical mountain –

Reference for Plas Brondanw:
Richard Haslam – *Clough Williams-Ellis*, 1996, pp.100-1.

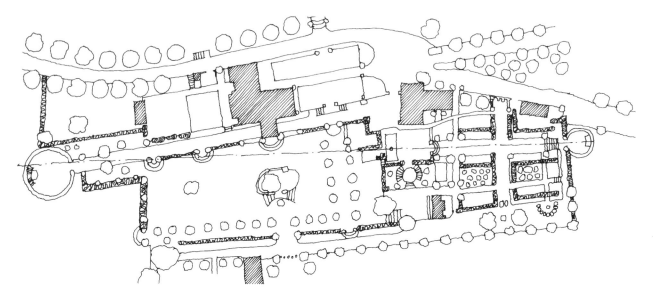

Cnicht – some miles to the north-east. This axis, established partly by the arrangement of hedges, and mainly by the alignment of openings in them, gives the garden a 'backbone'. Williams-Ellis was quite aware of the impressive power of this axis. Where you find it at the south-western end of the garden, he provided a seat onto which you can collapse in astonishment.

Hidcote Manor Garden in Gloucestershire (below) was developed over approximately the same period as Plas Brondanw, by Lawrence Johnston. Like the Williams-Ellis garden it consists of knots of room-like gardens, defined by high hedge walls, interspersed with larger spaces. Again there is an interplay between 'getting lost' and 'finding out where one is'. The house is the primary datum, as at Plas Brondanw, but in Hidcote, which is more extensive, one loses it more easily. The two principal 'reference spaces' at Hidcote are the large central lawn – 'The Theatre Lawn' – and the long, narrow grass pathway lined with high hedges known as 'The Long Walk'.

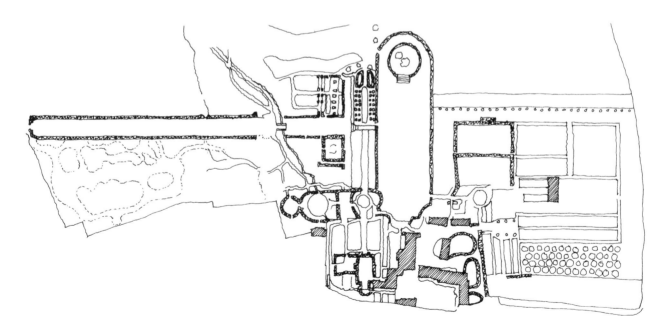

The city can be a maze. Part of the excitement of the old city of Jerusalem is that one can get lost in it. There are some significant landmarks – the Dome of the Rock is perhaps the most apparent on the plan (below) – and remnants of a Roman main street (the Cardo) have been uncovered, but generally the streets are narrow and their pattern is irregular. There are few places where one can see for a distance and get one's bearings. Unless one knows the city well, perhaps the most reliable reference is the outer wall; at least when one's

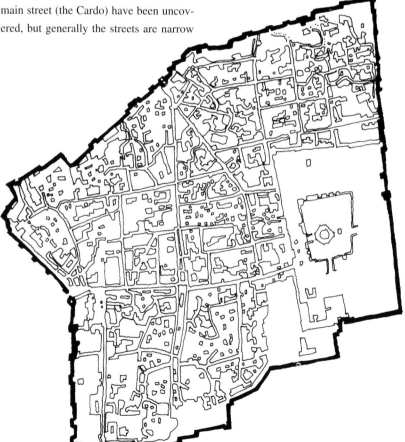

Jerusalem is a city in which it is easy to get lost. The street pattern is irregular and not orthogonal. There are strong landmarks, but the narrow streets mean that one can rarely see them from a distance, to help get one's bearings. Perhaps the strongest datum, most helpful in knowing where you are, is the outer wall.

wandering leads to it one has some clue as to where in the city one is.

The orthodox Roman garrison town was much more ordered. Its regular hierarchy of streets and the temple at its centre meant that it would probably have been very difficult to get lost. Directions would have been easy to give. The ordered layout would have contributed to the efficient running of the community. The plan created its own datum framework, within which everyone knew where they were.

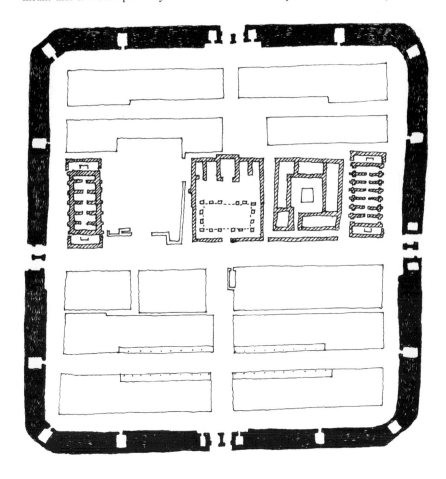

By contrast, the orthodox Roman garrison town is ordered and legible. It would have been difficult, if not impossible, to get lost in one. The regular pattern of streets, arranged orthogonally according to a strict hierarchy, makes the town's layout easy to read, even from eye-level.

The plan of Venice, set on its islands, suggests that the reverse S-shaped Grand Canal should act as a datum within the city, helping visitors to know where they are. To those moving about the city on the water it does to some extent provide a principal route to which the minor canals relate. But to those walking the city on foot, the Grand Canal is not a great deal of use as a datum. One is not able to walk along the side of very great lengths of it; the walls of the buildings come right up to the water's edge. When one penetrates the maze of streets one loses sight of the canal very quickly, and the irregularity of the street pattern makes it difficult to retain a sense of direction for very long.

Dubrovnik, by contrast, is an ancient walled city in which it is almost impossible to get lost. The plan (right) shows some of the reasons why. The principal of these is that the city has one main street, the

"... the shortest distance between two points in Esmeralda is not a straight line but a zigzag that ramifies in tortuous optional routes, the ways that open to each passerby are never two, but many..."

Italo Calvino, translated by William Weaver – *Invisible Cities*, 1972, p.88.

The Grand Canal in Venice acts as a more useful datum for those moving about the city on the water than it does for those on foot. One cannot walk very far along its edge, and the narrow streets mean that one loses sight of it quickly when one walks amongst the buildings.

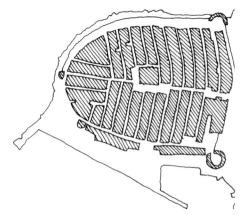

The fortified peninsular town of Korcula, on the Adriatic island of the same name, is in some ways a reverse of Dubrovnik. It is smaller, and the spine route is not so clear. Also, the secondary lanes descend, rather than ascend, from the axis of the town. The church stands at the centre, but the strongest datum, by which one knows where one is, is the sea, seen framed in narrow slices between the walls of the houses.

The Stradun is the backbone of the layout of Dubrovnik. It joins the main gateway to the harbour. Secondary streets run perpendicular to it, running uphill to the outer walls. The combination of clear, simple layout and level changes make it impossible to get lost.

Stradun, leading from its main gate to the harbour. Off this backbone run the ribs of the secondary lanes, laid out, for the most part, on a fairly regular orthogonal pattern. The Stradun runs along the lowest level of the city too; the lanes, in both directions, run uphill from it to the city walls, so that one always knows in which direction one must go to find the main street again.

There is enough irregularity in the city of Dubrovnik to prevent it becoming monotonous, but the regularity and clear hierarchy of the street system, defined by the walls of the buildings, make it a clearly legible city.

At each end of Dubrovnik's main street there is a small square. One is identified by a large circular fountain from which one can drink. The other, near the harbour gate, is slightly larger and dominated by a church. There is a concentration of the civic buildings of the city around this latter square, contributing to the ordered hierarchy and legibility of the plan.

In some cities the provision of a square or piazza is the strongest datum. The

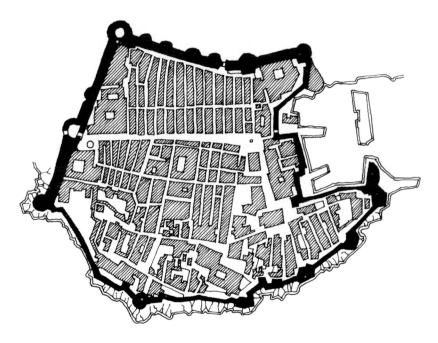

153

town of Pompeii was centred on its forum, dominated by the temple of Jupiter, providing a physical, political, and religious datum for the town.

The plans of Roman houses had their own internal hierarchy too. As has been noted in the chapter 'Enclosure' above, Greek and Roman town houses were generally enclosed within high walls to the street, with few windows to the outside. In this they were introverted and very private. Rooms were arranged around the periph-

The heart of Pompeii was its forum, an open space defined by the walls of the surrounding buildings, and providing a place of reference.

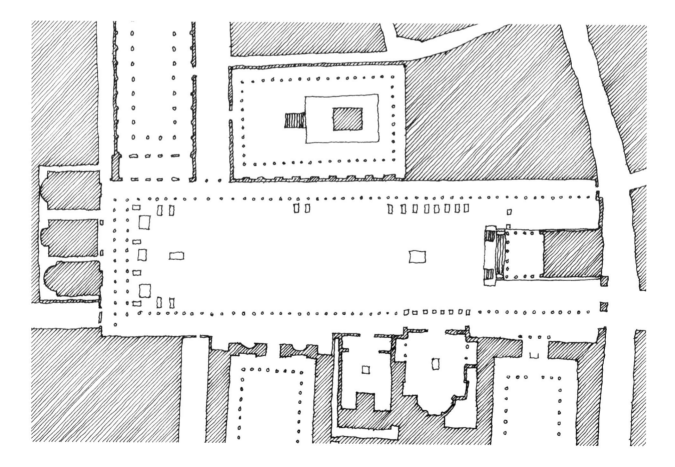

ery, opening onto a central court, or atrium. Below is the ground floor plan of the House of the Surgeon, in Pompeii. The atrium was the entrance hall and reception space, lit from the sky through an opening in the roof. Rainwater was collected in a pool,

alongside which was a stone table altar. This space may not have been the functional heart of the house, but it provided a datum to which all the other accommodation related.

Larger Roman houses often had more than one datum space, with different purposes and roles. The House of the Faun, also in Pompeii, has four, providing light, air, water, and green vegetation. The smallest is the entrance atrium. The largest, to the left of the plan, is the garden, enclosed like a medieval cloister by a high wall and peristylar colonnade. The combination of the small rooms and the larger sky-lit datum spaces provides a pattern of light and shade, as well as helping make the layout of the house easy to understand for the occupants.

This pattern, an atrium surrounded by smaller rooms, has been used by archi-

The houses in Pompeii had their own datum places within them, to which most of the rooms related. The House of the Surgeon (right) has an atrium at its heart, open to the sky. The House of the Faun (below) has a number of atria, and a large cloistered garden.

Reference for Greek and Roman houses: D.S. Robertson – Greek and Roman Architecture, 1969.

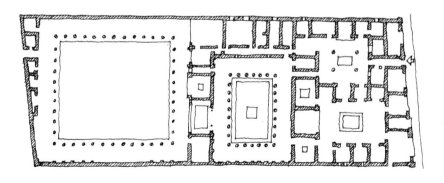

tects many times. The Casa del Fascio in Como, Italy, was designed by Giuseppe Terragni in the 1930s. He built it as a headquarters for Mussolini's Italian Fascist party. Terragni's building has a strongly 'Modern' appearance, with white walls and large areas of glass, under a flat roof and eaves line. But he consciously drew on ancient precedents in deciding on the architecture of its layout. He was particularly interested in ideas associated with buildings from great periods of the Italian past, including those of ancient Rome. The plans (below) illustrate some similarity with the Roman town house. The entrance leads into a central atrium, lit from the sky through the glass roof. All the smaller rooms, around the periphery of the building, relate to this central datum space. Also, it could be opened to the piazza in front of the building, for use when Fascist leaders spoke to political gatherings.

The Casa del Fascio in Como (below), designed by Giuseppe Terragni in the 1930s as headquarters for Mussolini's Italian Fascist party, has an atrium at its heart, which acts as a datum.

Reference for Terragni's Casa del Fascio:
Giorgio Ciucci – *Giuseppe Terragni : opera completa*, 1996.

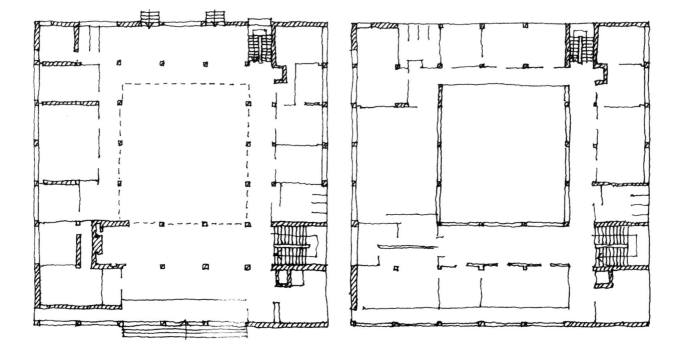

INHABITED WALL

INHABITED WALL

Discounting the imaginary walls we put up in our own minds, walls are solid, essentially. As has been said near the beginning of this *Notebook*, the surface of a wall, whether the natural wall of a cliff or cave or the mind-determined wall of a built enclosure or room, is an interface between space that can be occupied by life, and solid that cannot.

The surface of a wall is a barrier, but if the material is amenable, it is also an invitation to excavation, literally or metaphorically. Just as a sculptor's block of marble can be thought of as holding the potential form of the finished sculpture within it, so the solid substance of a wall can be thought of as holding the potential of usable space within it. It is perhaps usual to think of identifying places by building positive elements that manage space, but the space of a place can also be obtained by the negative process of subtraction, i.e. by taking material away rather than adding it.

Such 'mining' of space is of course not necessarily subject to the same constraints of the 'geometry of making' as space enclosed by 'additive' building. Space excavated from solid rock (or even the solid timber mass of a large tree) can be 'free' of structural disciplines that constrain the forms and dispositions of built

The trunk of the Baobab tree (right), which grows in Africa, can be large enough to excavate as a living space.

In many parts of the world the rock is soft enough to excavate to make troglodyte dwellings. The shape of 'mined' space is not necessarily subject to the same disciplines of the 'geometry of making' as that defined by built structures. The drawing (far right) shows the plan of some troglodyte dwellings excavated in Matamata, Tunisia.

walls and the roofs they might support, though this does not mean that they are also free of the influences of 'social' or 'ideal' geometries.

The excavation of solid rock to create space can have spiritual and religious meaning. You can perhaps imagine the effect on your emotions and aesthetic sensibilities of carving a space out of solid matter, into which one can remove oneself from the outside world. Exposure is replaced by protection. Some religions have believed that gods occupy rock, so exca-

vation can be be thought of as an attempt to get closer to, even inside, a deity.

In hot climates rocks moderate heat. An excavation can be a place to escape into shade away from strong summer sun. But heat stored in the rock can make the same place a warm haven on colder winter days.

Perhaps the most powerful character of excavated space is that it seems to create a place 'between', i.e. between the open space of the world (or universe) and the solidity of matter. An excavated space is both outside and inside the solid ma-

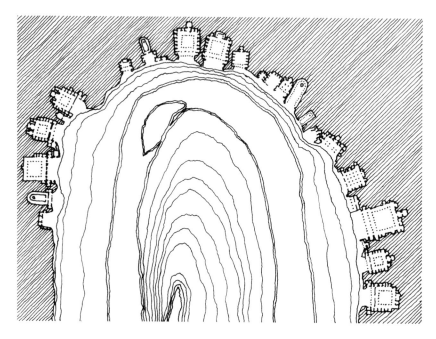

At Ajanta in India many shrines have been excavated out of the cliff walls of a ravine at the bend of a river. Together they constitute a perforated wall. The shrines occupy a space 'between' the open undefined space of the world and the solid matter of the earth, making a zone where space invades matter, and vice versa..

terial. Making it necessarily creates new surfaces between occupiable space and unoccupiable matter, but that space is different in that it is 'inside' the matter.

This sense of excavated space being in some sense a space 'between' is appreciable too when space is metaphorically 'excavated' out of the solid matter of built walls. It might be said that the walls and roof of a cell 'excavate' space from space, a particular defined space from general space. The material from which those walls are built then constitutes solid from which space can be regained.

The Broch of Mousa (below) is a fortified house in Scotland. Its walls are so thick that it was possible to form small rooms within them.

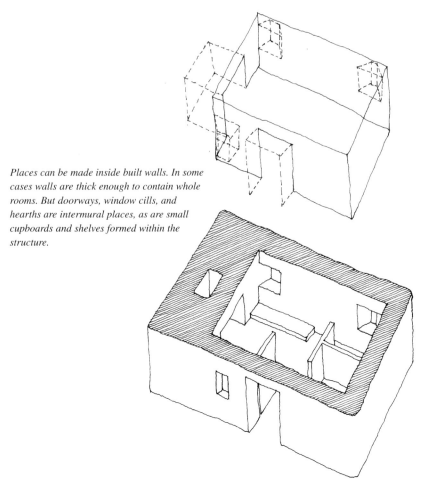

Places can be made inside built walls. In some cases walls are thick enough to contain whole rooms. But doorways, window cills, and hearths are intermural places, as are small cupboards and shelves formed within the structure.

Stone houses and cottages tend to have thick walls. The doorways and window in these walls make places themselves. The doorway becomes a porch. The window cills are deep enough for storage and display. The heart of the cottage, its hearth, is a place inside one of the walls.

Comlongan Castle, in Scotland, like the Broch of Mousa, has walls that are thick enough to contain rooms. Some of these intermural rooms are contained completely within the walls, some are open to the central hall, like large window places in which one can sit. The two stairs are completely within the walls. The composition creates a hierarchy of subsidiary rooms around a principal space – annexes to the hall.

This composition of subsidiary spaces within the walls of a principal space

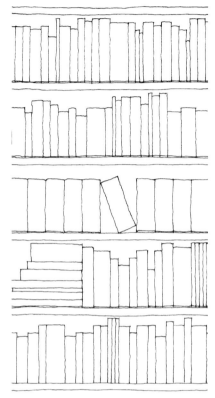

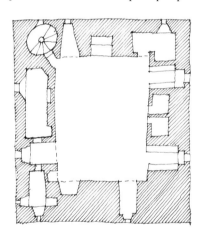

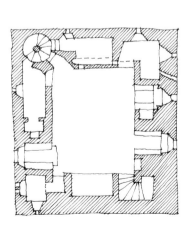

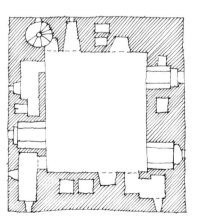

On each of its four floors, Comlongan Castle in Scotland has one main room. All the subsidiary rooms are contained within the thickness of the castle's walls. These subsidiary rooms also have smaller places 'excavated' out of their walls – cupboards, shelves, window places, seats.

Bookshelves can be thought of as inhabited walls. As well as being used for storing books, in libraries they also often help to organise space. The life that inhabits them is the life contained in the many books they hold....

is a theme frequently encountered in works of architecture of all historical periods. It involves thought about how space use interacts with structure.

In the Celsian Library (below), built at Ephesus in the second century, the walls are 'excavated' to accommodate storage niches for the scrolls, and to provide surfaces on which they could be read.

The structural order of Albi Cathedral (right) in south-western France helps expand the walls to create many side chapels off the central nave.

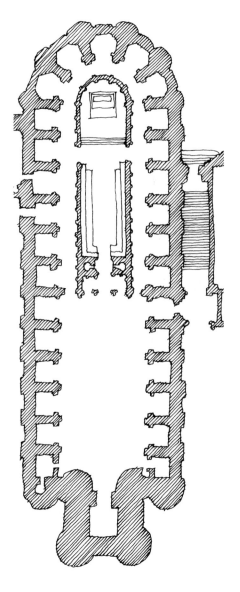

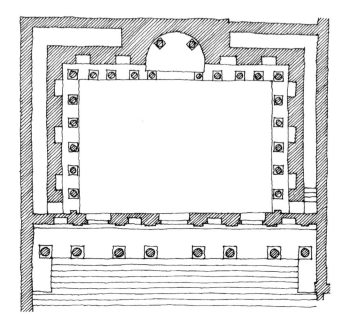

In towns and cities the walls of streets and squares are inhabited. The houses, shops, and other buildings form the walls of the public spaces.

Sometimes, as in the 'Rows' of Chester (bottom), the walls are 'excavated' to provide public walkways. In this example the pedestrian walkways are raised

Many Saxon villages in Transylvania have fortified churches. Villagers could take refuge within the protected compound in times of attack. They stored food and lived in the...

In Bedford Square, London (above), the inhabited façades of the town houses make the walls of a large urban room. The rooms of the house, with their carefully proportioned windows, are like theatre boxes looking out onto the public stage.

above the level of the street. They reach quite deeply into the mass of the buildings that line the streets, and break down the division of public street and private interior. They provide a sheltered transition between outside and inside.

In Bedford Square, London, the walls of the houses define the larger stage of the public square.

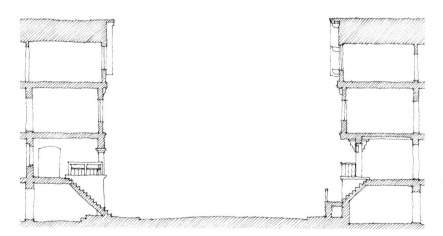

In Chester's 'Rows', elevated pedestrian walkways are 'excavated' out of the façades of the buildings, providing a space between inside and outside.

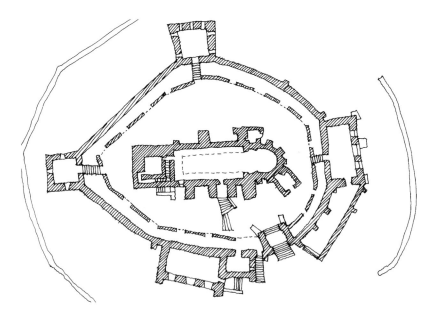

... inhabited wall around the church. Above are the section and the plan of the Deutsch-Weißkirch at Viscri.

Reference for Transylvania's fortified churches:
Herman Fabini – *Atlas der siebenbürgisch-sächsischen Kirchenburgen und Dorfkirchen*, 1999.

The theatres in which Shakespeare's plays were performed in the seventeenth century were developed from courtyards, in which drama had previously been performed. In such courtyard performances the audience inhabited the walls of the surrounding building, watching through win-

This drawing shows a section through the theatre, including the stage. Behind the stage is another inhabited wall. This wall provides the backdrop for the action. It also incorporates windows, balconies and doorways that can be used as part of the scenery for the drama.

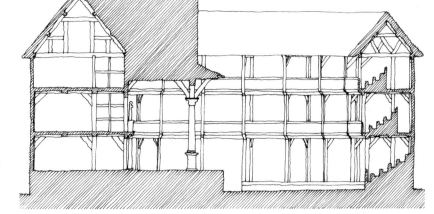

The walls of the Globe Theatre in London are inhabited by the audience. The wall behind the stage can also be inhabited, providing places inside it which can be used as part of the scenery for the action of the play.

Reference for the Globe Theatre, London:
Ronnie Mulryne and Margaret Shewring (editors) – *Shakespeare's Globe Rebuilt*, 1997.

dows. In the purpose-made courtyard theatres, such as the Globe Theatre, London (above), the circle of walls enclosing the performance place was expanded inwards to accommodate the seating. When full of people, mesmerised by the actors on stage, the three tiers of galleries make an affecting example of an inhabited wall. It is almost a wall of people.

The courtyards of courtyard houses are usually formed of inhabited walls. Their underlying form derives from a realisation that wrapping a building around in a square or circle makes a usable protected unroofed space within. Passing through this inhabited wall from outside to the courtyard, which is often used as a datum space, makes a transition from public to private.

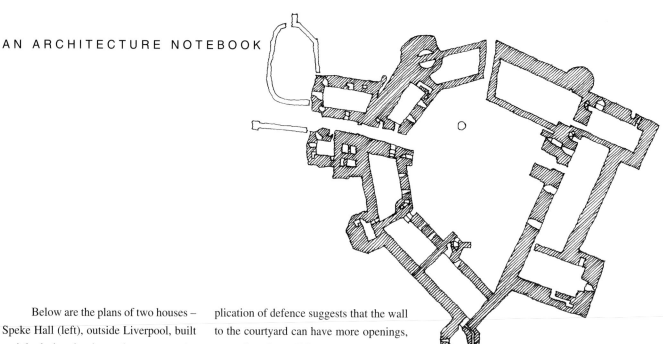

Below are the plans of two houses – Speke Hall (left), outside Liverpool, built mainly during the sixteenth century, and a patio house in Tapiola, Finland, designed by Pentti Ahola and built in the 1960s. These two houses are from different countries and periods of history, but their plans are organised in similar ways. Both enclose a courtyard with an 'inhabited wall' of accommodation. The character of the wall that divides the 'inhabited wall' from the outside world is, in such examples, often different from that which divides the accommodation from the courtyard. The implication of defence suggests that the wall to the courtyard can have more openings, more glass, less solidity than the outer wall. The relationship with the 'inside' is different from the 'outside'. The courtyard also acts as a datum space so that wherever you are in the house you have a reference point by which you know where you are. The minds that determined these plans both positioned the circulation space – in Speke Hall a corridor, in the Tapiola house, an implied route – next to the courtyard.

Medieval castles often used the idea of the inhabited wall. Their primary archi-

The medieval castle of Llawhaden in Wales is essentially an area of ground protected against enemies by a wall. Accommodation was built along the inside of this defensive wall.

Speke Hall (left) and a patio house in Finland (right) illustrate the architectural theme of an 'inhabited wall' around a courtyard.

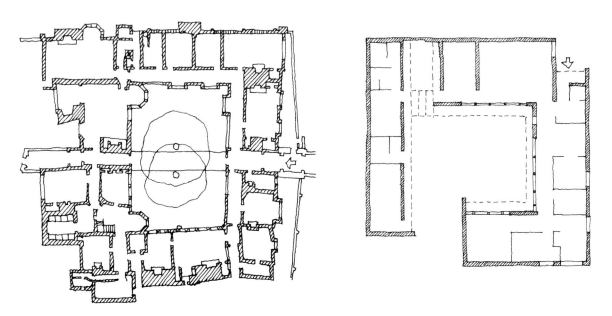

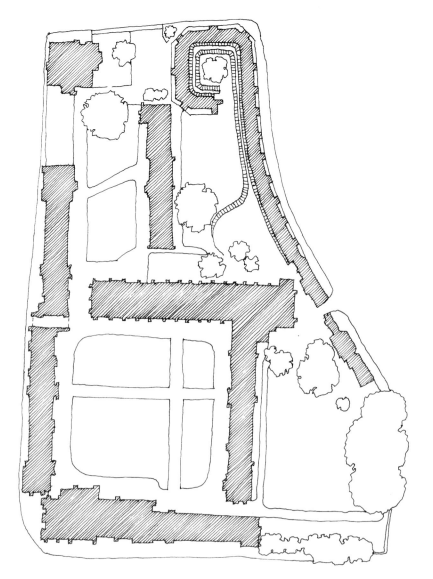

tectural element was the defensive curtain wall surrounding the protected area of the castle. It was sensible to use this wall as one of the walls of the living accommodation.

The idea of the defensive 'inhabited wall' is evident too in Ralph Erskine's design for housing in Byker near Newcastle upon Tyne – known as the Byker Wall. It was 'defended' by a long, snaking wall of apartments all along one side of the site, not against 'enemies', but against the noise of traffic. As in the courtyard houses opposite, this 'inhabited wall' has more openness to the inside than to the outside.

Architects in the twentieth century explored the relationship between accom-

The buildings of Keble College, Oxford, are like 'inhabited walls' defining the external spaces. The curved building at the top right of the site plan (above) was designed by Ahrends Burton and Koralek in the 1970s. The other buildings date from the nineteenth century, and were designed by William Butterfield.

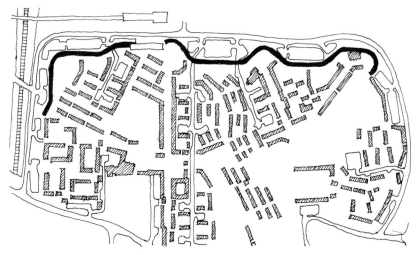

The Byker Wall (right) protected the housing estate with an 'inhabited wall' which had an outside wall that was well insulated against noise, and a more open inner wall.

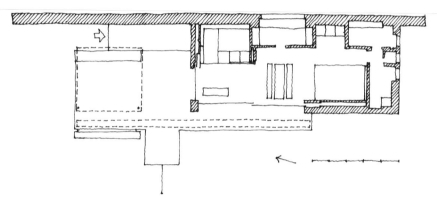

Reference for Minoletti's weekend villa on Lake Como:
G.E. Kidder Smith - *Italy Builds*, Architectural Press, 1954, pp.134-5.

modation and the wall in many different ways. Some, like Giulio Minoletti and Jorn Utzon, have used a single straight wall as the starting point for a house. Minoletti's weekend villa on Lake Como in Italy (above) was built in 1940. The house by Utzon (below) is in Finland. Both are walls with accommodation attached to one side. In both the wall directs the house, in the first case to the view across the lake, and in the second to the sun. Subsidiary accommodation is lined up against the wall.

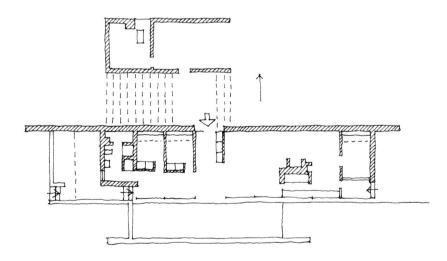

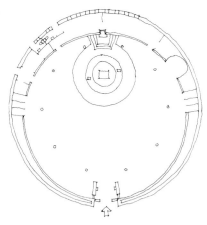

The plan of this church in Ireland is formed of two circles, one off-centre inside the other. The space between constitutes an 'inhabited wall', used for the subsidiary places. It is the Church of St Aengus, Burt in County Donegal. It was designed by Liam McCormick and built in 1965.

Reference for the Church of St Aengus:
Becker, Olley and Wang – *Twentieth Century Architecture, Ireland*, 1997, p.131.

In the Marvin House Edward Cullinan attached a large lightweight living space to a heavy 'inhabited wall' of other accommodation. The 'inhabited wall' is built in masonry, the living space in timber. The 'wall' is divided into the rooms that require more privacy – bedrooms, bathroom etc.

Reference for Marvin House:
John Donat (editor) – *World Architecture 1*, Studio Vista, 1964, pp.48-9.

Liam McCormick designed the Church of St Aengus in the 1960s. He wanted the building to be circular on the outside and have a circular main space inside, and yet he had to accommodate other spaces too, which could have diluted this idea. His solution (top left) was to make two circular walls, not concentric, and use the space between as an inhabited wall.

Edward Cullinan designed the Marvin House (left), which was built in California, in the late 1950s. This house has accommodation attached to a principal wall too. But in this case the principal wall is itself 'inhabited' by subsidiary accommodation. The wall that outlines the 'inhabited wall' in plan is turned back on itself a number of times so that the rooms within it themselves have walls 'inhabited' by cupboards and bath alcoves. At the doorways these returns also create transitions between the main living space and the more private rooms inside the wall.

Cullinan created an interplay between the two parts of the house by making the 'inhabited wall' of heavy materials, and the attached accommodation of light timber. The external effect is to suggest a heavy, very thick block wall, with lightweight accommodation attached. In this instance the line of the best view from the

169

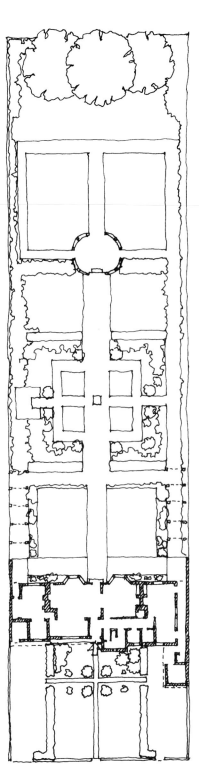

house is parallel rather than perpendicular to the principal wall.

Sometimes a house can be an 'inhabited wall', dividing two outside spaces.

The house and garden on the right were designed by H. Baillie Scott just before the First World War. They are at 48 Storey Way in Cambridge. The house itself acts as an inhabited wall between the front garden open to the roadway, and the more private back garden. The house and garden were designed together, with the outside spaces given equivalent importance to the internal rooms, and with correspondences made between them. For example, the central axis of the whole design stretches from the front boundary, right through the house, and to the end of the garden. It defines a pathway and a line of sight. As one enters the front door, when the garden door is open, one sees a framed view of the pathway lined with plants.

Baillie Scott experimented with walls in various ways. He explored the potential of spaces between inside and outside, expanding the zone of the wall to accommodate smaller spaces which made rooms more complex than boxes. He made agglomerations of many smaller 'places': places to sit, places to eat.... He built a house for himself in the early 1890s. He

Baillie Scott's design for a house at 48 Storey Way in Cambridge makes an 'inhabited wall' dividing the front from the rear garden.

Reference for Baillie Scott's houses:
Diane Haigh – *Baillie Scott, the artistic house*, 1995.

Baillie Scott played with the zone between inside and outside. In his houses he sometimes pushed small spaces outside the main structure of the house to create bay windows, or pulled walls inside the line of the structure of the roof to make porches or verandahs.

called it the Red House, partly in homage to the house designed thirty years earlier at Bexley Heath by Philip Webb for William Morris. The combination of Hall, Dining Room, and Drawing Room in this house is not a series of three rooms, but more a 'flow' of space. The plan of the ground floor is illustrated below. The plan is interesting too because of the way he pulls and pushes the walls of this space. In two places he pushes bay windows outside the line of the wall to make sitting spaces. In another place he pulls the wall inside the line of the overhanging roof to create an outside sitting place. The fireplace of the Drawing Room is pushed outside the structure of the roof above, to make an

ingle around the fire. The drawing on the right below shows some of the games Baillie Scott played with the wall, and the zone between inside and outside. The result is a rich composition of space and light, making many small places which people can relate to and use.

Baillie Scott's 'games' were to do with exploring relationships, and blurring the division, between inside space and outside. They were also to do with testing and breaking the direct relationship between a wall's structural role in supporting the sheltering roof and its role in defining space. They constituted an argument that the two roles could perhaps be separated, with a consequent enrichment of architecture.

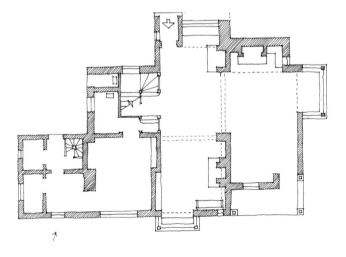

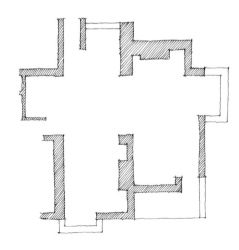

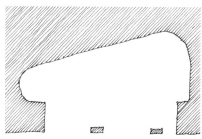

In the abbey church attached to the monastery of La Tourette near Lyon in southern France, Le Corbusier thought of outside space in a different way. Its interior is like a formalised primitive landscape of cliffs, sky and sun, with an uneven ground surface. In this he implied that the interiors of ancient cathedrals could be seen in the same sort of way, reinvigorating their ancestry in natural settings.

One of the principal elements in the abbey church at La Tourette is the south chapel. It opens like a cave in the stark cliff of the south wall of the church. Its plan form, though not attempting to be artifi-

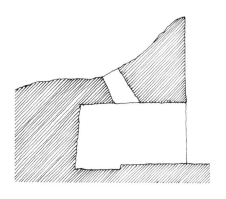

cial in nature, avoids the orthogonal. It has roof lights in raised 'funnels' that suggest to the eye in the interior that the fabric of the 'cave' is much thicker and heavier than it actually is. In this Le Corbusier 'excavated' the cavern-like south chapel out of outside space as if it was solid matter. The effect is greatly to reinforce the sense that the nave of the church is itself deeply embedded in solid matter.

If one looks beneath the ornamentation, what Le Corbusier did at La Tourette can be seen to be not so different from the situation in which chapels are embedded in the fabric of Renaissance churches.

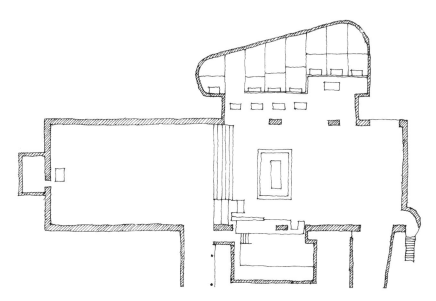

The south chapel of the abbey church at the monastery of La Tourette (left) is 'carved' out of the 'solid mass' of outside space.

Many churches have this character. Il Gesù in Rome (right) is like a cave with many side caverns excavated from undifferentiated space.

Il Gesù in Rome was designed by Vignola and built in the late sixteenth century. Its transepts and sanctuary, as well as the many small chapels, are like caves excavated into the walls of the nave.

The implication in these cases is that inhabited space can be considered as being 'excavated' from non-specific space, and that walls are instruments of excavation.

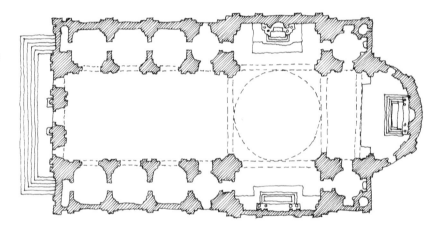

Architects sometimes make walls appear more substantial than they are, maybe to increase the apparent solidity of their buildings. The most appropriate place to accomplish this illusion is around openings. In his Villa Coucou, built in Tokyo in 1957, Takemasa Yoshizaka provided surrounds

he formed a niche for the lectern, the visual effect of which was to suggest a thick and heavy wall. And at the bottom right-hand corner of the plan he provided the small window with a thickness-implying surround. Wherever one might be able directly to perceive the actual thickness of the wall,

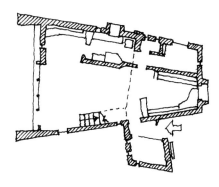

outside some of the small windows to suggest from the inside that the walls of the house were thicker than they actually were.

And, as has been noted in *Analysing Architecture*, Erik Gunnar Asplund manipulated the apparent thickness of the walls of his Woodland Chapel at the Woodland Crematorium in Stockholm. At the door he returned the walls to make it seem as if the wall through which you pass as you enter is a few feet rather than a few inches thick. At the other end of the chapel

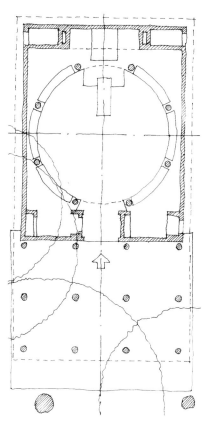

In the Woodland Chapel (left) Asplund manipulated the layout of the walls to make them seem to be thicker than they are actually are.

Reference for the Woodland Chapel: Caroline Constant – *The Woodland Chapel: towards a spiritual landscape*, 1994.

In his design for the Assembly Rooms in Glasgow (right) Robert Adam wanted the individual shapes of the rooms to take precedence over walls with regular thicknesses. In some places he managed to arrange things so that the wall thickness did not become excessive. In others he used thick walls to accommodate smaller rooms 'excavated' from within them.

Reference for the Glasgow Assembly Rooms: Joseph and Anne Rykwert – *The Brothers Adam: the men and the style*, 1985, p.193.

Asplund manipulated the situation to make the wall appear much thicker than it actually is.

In many buildings the walls are of uniform thickness. Built of a regular ma-

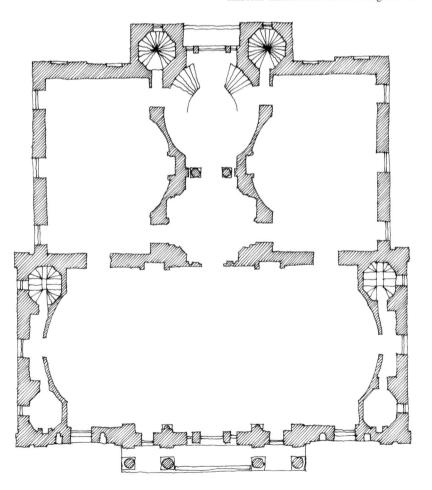

terial, the sides are parallel. This happens when adjacent rooms are rectangular, but sometimes architects want to give priority to giving rooms non-rectangular shapes. This can usually only be accomplished by allowing the walls to vary in thickness. Sometimes this results in walls being in part of such great thickness that small rooms can be 'excavated' within them.

In his first-floor plan for the Assembly Rooms in Glasgow (1796-8) Robert Adam wanted an oval stair hall flanked by rooms with large apses. He managed to arrange these so that not too much space was wasted in the walls. Elsewhere he filled the *poche* between the curved ends of the large ballroom and the rectangular outer surfaces of the building's walls with octagonal staircases and small rooms. He also increased the apparent thickness of the external wall of the stair hall with two stair towers, and layered the wall over the main entrance with paired columns either side of an Italian window.

Adam, like many architects, created niches in walls too, in which pieces of sculpture could be displayed. The effect is to subvert the deathly solidity of the wall by giving it relief. The niches frame the exhibited objects, just as the rooms frame the lives of their occupants. Both become

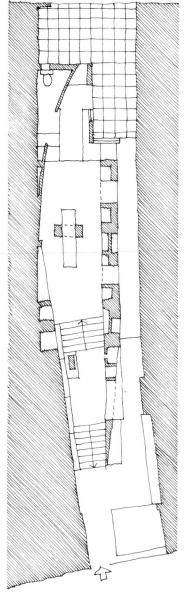

In his design for the Wilson and Gough Gallery (right), David Chipperfield used one principal wall to divide the irregular given space. He 'inhabited' this wall, and parts of the two side walls, with exhibition cases.

Reference for the Wilson and Gough Gallery: Domus, May 1989, pp.66-70.

stages, one occupied by frozen action, the other by life. The juxtaposition camouflages the wall. It also juxtaposes the in-

animate statuary (memorials, trophies and manifestations of wealth) with living people. There is a poetic relationship between

Niches allow walls to be inhabited by the dead representations of living things, juxtaposed with the life occupying the space adjacent.

the 'inhabitation' of the wall and that of the space it defines.

In the Maison de Verre in Paris (1931, below) the architect Pierre Chareau expanded just about every wall to provide usable space. The house is squeezed into a tight closed courtyard. The party wall at the top of this second-floor plan is one long line of cupboards, wash spaces, niches, shelves.... There is hardly a wall in the house that isn't 'inhabited' in some way. The walls between the bedrooms and the gallery are wardrobes. Even the balustrades between the galleries and the open triple-height space are used for display cases. In this house the walls are not occupied so much by dead representations of life as by the latent accoutrements of life: 'dormant' clothes and books; service pipes; washing, dressing... preparations for life rather than life itself.

All the examples given so far in this chapter have been of walls expanded to make places for purposes. These might be

In the Maison de Verre Pierre Chareau used nearly every wall for useful space. They accommodate cupboards, wardrobes, wash spaces, bookcases, display cases....

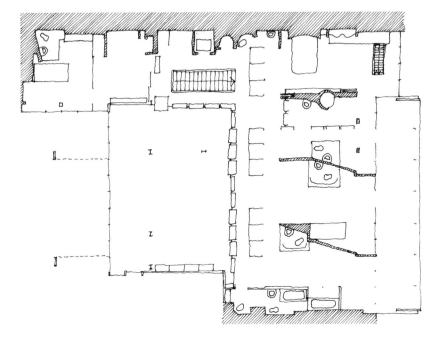

places for sitting or sleeping, places for storage and for washing, places for display, places for worship....

Architects have expanded walls also for aesthetic and symbolic reasons.

It seems that early temples in the eastern Mediterranean were simple cells: walls, roof, doorway... and perhaps a porch. The drawing on the right shows such a simple temple building, on the island of Crete, at Prinia.

Later temples were more elaborate. First they were given more regular rows of columns on the front, veiling the entrance. Then their form was 'balanced' with a matching row of columns providing a pseudo-porch at the rear of the building.

Eventually temple cells were shrouded completely by rows of columns around the whole building. The Temple of Ceres at Paestum (right) is one of many examples. A simple cell temple with a four-columned porch is surrounded by a rectangular enclosure of columns. The roof, of course, reached to the outer columns.

These rows of columns, especially those to the sides and rear of the temple, could not be said to be there to make a place or series of places; the space between them and the cell of the temple has no clear definite purpose. The reason for their being

there seems to have been to ornament the temple, perhaps to give it a more 'equal' appearance on all of it four sides, and perhaps to modify the appearance of the side and rear walls, which otherwise would appear blank and boring. The effect is to expand the zone of the wall, subverting its

Early temples were little more than simple cells consisting of walls, doorway, roof and perhaps a porch. Later ones were surrounded with columns to veil the blankness of the side and rear walls.

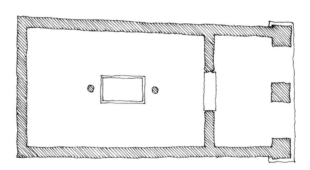

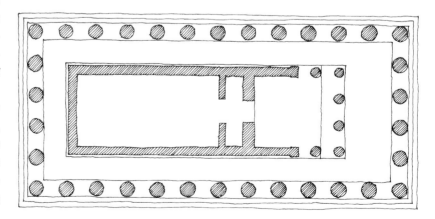

uncompromising solidity, creating a richer mix of rhythm, light and shade.

In some temples this device was used internally as well as externally. Rows of columns were built parallel to the cell's side walls. Presumably these too were there to soften the blankness of the side walls (perhaps more so than to provide intermediate

the interior is in no way reduced, but the appearance of exclusiveness is modified. Also, the apparent size of the building is greatly increased without increasing the corresponding size of the interior space. A relatively intimate interior is maintained embedded in a substantially larger building. Presumably the space within the for-

The columns of classical Greek temples expanded the zone of their walls, not to create places for use but for aesthetic reasons. The columns soften the harsh blankness of the walls, both externally and internally, making a richer pattern of light and shade, and replacing a flat surface with a modifying rhythm.

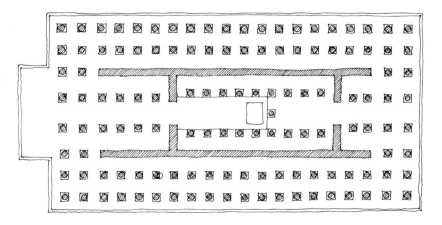

Reference for Greek temples:
A.W. Lawrence – *Greek Architecture*, 1957.

support for the roof), creating a more 'mysterious' interior.

The Temple of Artemis at Ephesus (above) was provided with two rows of columns around the exterior of the cell, and one row on each side of its interior. The result is that the principal enclosing wall of the cell is deep in a forest of columns that soften its blankness. The security of

est of columns was used for some things, perhaps for quiet conversation, but the zone of the wall is fringed... expanded not primarily to make places for use but for aesthetic and for symbolic reasons.

The section through the Temple of Apollo at Didyma (overleaf) clearly shows that an important role of the walls and columns of ancient temples was to screen the sacred place, image, statue, or even a smaller temple from public view. In this instance this screening purpose seems to have been stronger than that of protecting the sacred focus from the weather by supporting a roof. The drawings below show how the walls and their rows of columns created a solid veil and a curtain around the small temple at the focus of the building, set in its pit, separating its sacred circle of presence from everywhere else, except, in this case, the sky. There are no internal rows of columns, but the internal surface of the curtain wall has representations of columns carved into it, relieving its blankness, and perhaps suggesting that the architect would have liked the sacred enclosure to have consisted only of columns, but also realised that security, privacy and seclusion required a wall.

The walls of some of the cathedrals of the Middle Ages are expanded more greatly, more dramatically, and with richer effect than those of ancient Greek temples.

The central nave of Chartres Cathedral (opposite) is its main space. It is defined, essentially, by two parallel side walls supporting the vault of the roof. But the blank solidity of this wall is subverted in a number of ways. At the ground level the walls are replaced by rows of columns supporting arches which support the wall above. These columns allow access into the side aisles of the cathedral, creating an expanded wall, and camouflaging the final enclosure of the inside of the building.

Above the aisle arcades the walls are pierced by windows made as large as the builders dared. These windows reduce the blankness of the wall, allowing (as the in-

The walls of the temple of Apollo at Didyma are not there to shelter the small inner temple from the weather, but rather to protect its privacy, to preserve its sacred separation from the ordinary world. The expanded wall surrounded by rows of columns form a curtain and a veil around that special separated enclosure.

The walls of Chartres Cathedral are expanded to create aisles alongside the nave, but also to strengthen upper walls pierced by large windows. The result is a rich, intricate, organic and sculptural form.

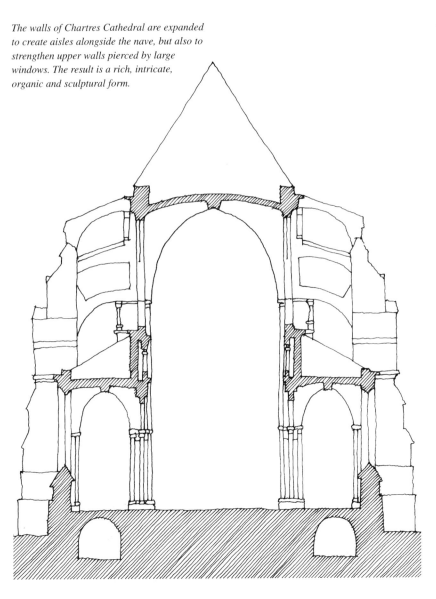

terpretation goes) the light of life, or 'after-life', to shine through the wall 'of death'. The structural consequences of these large openings meant that all sorts of props and buttresses were needed to maintain stability. To avoid interrupting and compromising the all-important internal space these were positioned exclusively on the exterior of the building. The result is a building which, from outside, appears not to have solid walls, but which is formed of a rich and intricate sculptural composition of virtuoso stonework, with soaring pinnacles and buttresses flying in every direction. The spaces within this expanded wall, excepting the aisle, are not intended for occupation or use. They may be the result of the practical need to support a wall with large openings, but they create a building with the apparent organic power of a living organism.

The expansion and manipulation of the zone of the wall for effect is rich ground for architectural exploration and adventure.

The Kaleva Church at Tampere in Finland (overleaf) was designed by Raili

Reference for Chartres Cathedral:
John James – *The Contractors of Chartres* (two volumes), 1981.

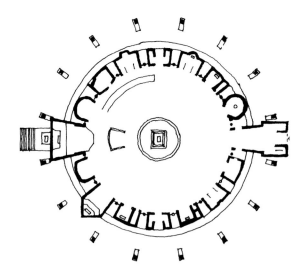

Paatelainen and Raima Pietilä, and built in 1966. The nave of the church is defined by tall vertical walls, rising to a flat ceiling and roof. The walls do not make a 'parallel wall' space but are arranged irregularly around a space with a plan shaped like a kite. The blank solidity of the walls that define this space is diluted by their being divided into fragments curved, concave, so that they stand like huge roughly shaped columns. The tall, thin crevice spaces between these 'columns' allow light into the space, reflecting off the faceted surfaces of the walls. Some of the spaces between are also used... the sanctuary occupies a small group of them at the sharp end of the 'kite' and, to the side, the choir seats rise into one space, like the floor of a cave disappearing behind a bend in the rock. From outside the effect is different: the walls that were convex on the inside are concave, no longer 'columns' but 'buttresses', with the slivers of glass hidden in their recesses.

For the most part Paatelainen and Pietilä kept the surfaces of their walls clear of decoration and ornamentation, to em-

The Metropolitan Cathedral of Christ the King in Liverpool is a circular space, focused on the altar at the centre, outlined by a ring of small chapels. The cathedral was designed by Frederick Gibberd and built in 1967.

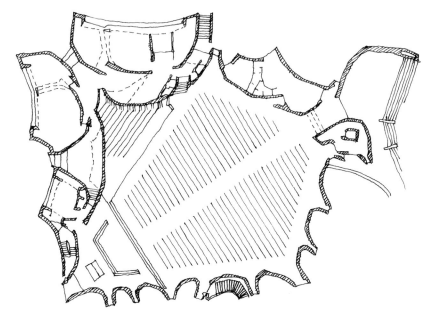

The Kaleva church is a reinterpretation of the relation between internal columns and external buttresses in church architecture. It also evokes the free organic form of the natural cave, but abstracts it into a subtle sculptural form. The expanded walls manage space and reflect light.

Reference for the Kaleva church:
Egon Tempel – *Finnish Architecture Today*, 1968, pp.173-5.

phasise their role in the manipulation of space and reflection of light. Narciso Tomé's Transparente in the cathedral of Toledo (1732, left) takes effect from the dramatic manipulation of space and from the reflection of light. Its surfaces are also encrusted with ornamentation, decoration, and statuary. The section, rather like that of the south chapel of Le Corbusier's abbey church at La Tourette, illustrates the use of the expanded wall to suggest cave-like space excavated not out of solid matter but out of general space. The expanded surfaces of the walls accommodate a whole culture of images, symbols, memorials, reminders, prayers, gospels, testaments, lessons, warnings, reassurances.... It is no wonder that in such a place it is easy to forget that there is such a thing as a simple, straightforward, uncompromising and final wall.

Baroque architects of the eighteenth century wanted to subvert the blank solidity of the wall as much as any architects ever. The Vierzehnheiligen ('fourteen saints') church near Bamberg in Germany

Reference for the Transparente in Toledo Cathedral:
Nikolaus Pevsner – *An Outline of European Architecture*, 1945, p.140.

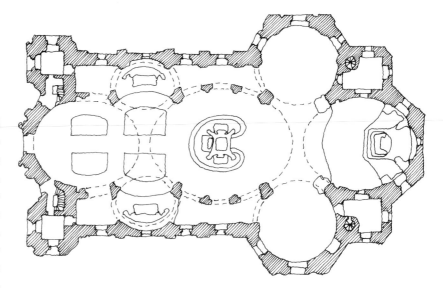

was designed by Balthasar Neumann, and built in the middle of the eighteenth century. Although the plan drawing suggests the walls of the church are solid enough, their arrangement and decoration, and the reflection of light from hidden sources, turn them more into a composition of colour, shade and brightness. The expansion of the walls inwards to define oval spaces with columns greatly reduces the apparent solidity of the division of the inside from the outside, creating an illusion of almost infinite space.

Le Corbusier expanded the walls of his chapel at Ronchamp for various reasons. In some places it was to reflect hidden sources of light, as in Baroque churches. He did it also to make small cavern-like spaces off the main 'cave' of the chapel.

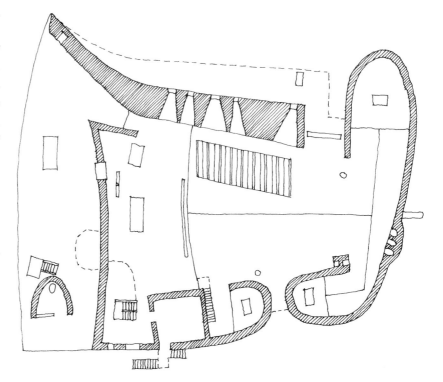

Reference for Vierzehnheiligen church:
Nikolaus Pevsner – *An Outline of European Architecture*, 1945, p.146.

Reference for the chapel at Ronchamp:
W. Boesiger – *Le Corbusier: œuvre complète (Volume 5) 1946-1952*, 1995, pp.72-84.

SOUND, HEAT, LIGHT

SOUND, HEAT, LIGHT

One day you might walk into a cathedral, out of curiosity, to look at what is there. But it may turn out that the most powerful impression is one made on a sense other than sight. Perhaps an alto is rehearsing a Bach cantata. The beautiful sound echoes around the hard stone walls.

If you visit the remains of the ancient city of Petra, in Jordan, on a cool day in winter you can experience a strange effect. As you enter some of the rock-cut chambers you feel the air is warm. The red walls of rock have stored the long months of intense summer heat, and are now radiators.

Walking around a troglodyte village in the Loire, on a hot French summer day... you wander into one of the dwellings and find a well shaft stretching from the water below to the ground surface some feet or metres above. There is a hatch allowing the occupants of the cave house to draw water. But the strongest aesthetic impression is of the sunlight on the texture of the rough stone walls of the shaft.

Walls contribute to the identity of places by the way they obscure, absorb, reflect, transmit... sound, heat and light. Maybe, in cold climates, the principal reason for walls has been to keep out the cold, or rather to keep in warmth. This, in early dwellings, had the disadvantage of also keeping out the light, or keeping (their occupants) in the dark, so there is, recognisable in the historical continuum of architecture, a progressive 'balancing act' between heat retention and light admission... ranging from the pitch-black caves of prehistory, to the almost totally glazed buildings of 'Modernism' which could become over-hot in the sunlight and very cold on a winter's night. In hot climates the walls that kept out cold also kept out excessive light, but when glass walls were adopted they could allow a combination of overheating and excess light. Mechanical ventilation, air-conditioning, and heating systems were used to supplement the effectiveness of walls, or the problems caused by glass walls.

There is a huge literature on these issues, born of much scientific research. There is room in this short chapter to consider briefly only some of the many ways in which walls affect and interplay with sound, heat and light.

Sound

Through history the wall has had a direct engagement with issues of heat and light. Its relations with sound have perhaps been

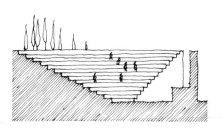

The wall (skene) behind the performers in an ancient Greek amphitheatre played a part in helping the audience hear what the actors were saying, by reflecting sound back towards them.

more esoteric... concerned with maintaining quiet places such as libraries and examination halls, places which require acoustic privacy such as counselling chambers and recording studios, and places where the quality of sound is important such as theatres and concert halls. In all these the wall is an essential instrument.

Walls relate to sound in different ways. They reflect sound, in ways which depend on the surface of the wall. The surfaces of the walls of a space affect its acoustic identity: hard surfaces give a harsh acoustic which, if the space is large, becomes echoey; soft, absorbent surfaces give a dead acoustic.

Walls can focus or dissipate sound. A sound made at one focus of an eliptical space will be focused, by the walls, at the other focus.

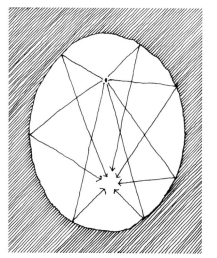

Eliptical and semicircular spaces can reflect sound, concentrating it at focal points.

If you stand at the focus of a semi-circular space and make a noise, it will seem much louder than to someone not at the focus, because of the reflections from the walls.

Likewise, if you stand at the centre of one of the great Greek amphitheatres, such as Epidavros, and stamp your foot on

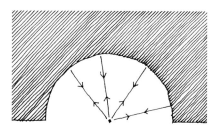

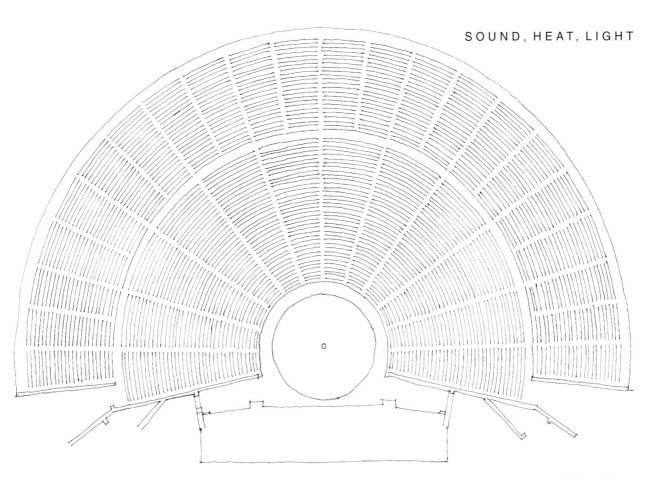

Whereas the circular form of a Greek amphitheatre (above), when empty, reflects sound back to the orkestra...

... the reflective surfaces in Hans Scharoun's Philharmonie in Berlin (below) are canted to dissipate the sound of the orchestra throughout the audience.

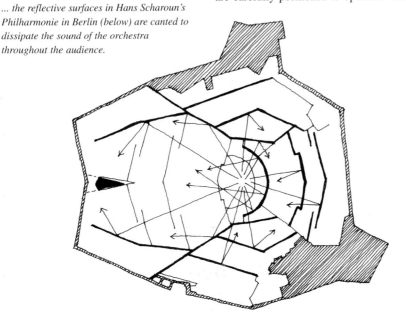

the stone pavement or clap your hands, you will hear the rapid-fire echoes from the 'wall' of each step in turn.

The front walls of the 'terraces' of Hans Scharoun's Philharmonie in Berlin are carefully positioned to optimise 'first reflections' of the sound of the orchestra to the audience, without creating places where the sound is particularly focused. The walls are canted, vertically as well as in the horizontal dimension, to dissipate sound through the space without causing disruptive echoes. The 'fin' wall at the back of the audience, triangular in plan (and coloured black in the drawing), occupies one possible focus of sound from the orchestra, and, by doing so, breaks it up by reflecting sound away.

Walls also transmit sound through their fabric, or allow it to pass through them by vibration. Sound passing through the walls of a space affects its character and its sense of privacy. Thin walls between hotel rooms give rise to their own problems... maybe the snoring of one guest will disturb the sleep of others. Excess noise from outside

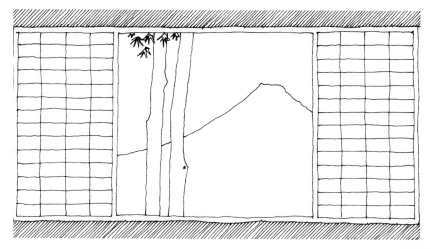

a meeting room will make concentration difficult and affect the effectiveness of the room in fulfilling its function.

Sometimes it has been the thinness of a wall that has been used to preserve privacy. Rooms in Japanese houses, in gardens or landscape settings, were built with very thin paper walls, and large opening screens, so that the presence of an eavesdropper outside could be easily sensed by those wishing to preserve the privacy of their conversations inside.

Some specialist rooms, for experiments, have been built in ways that reduce both reflected and transmitted sound to a minimum, almost nil. To achieve this, layers of wall are needed, fitted with sound-absorbent material.

Some Japanese walls were made of paper, thin enough for people talking inside to hear if there was someone listening outside.

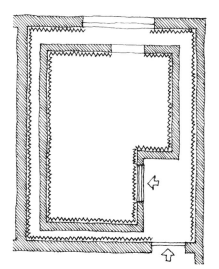

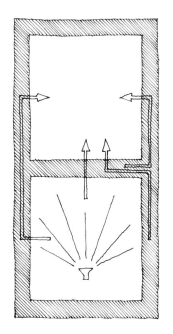

The walls of recording studios are essential to their function. When Broadcasting House (opposite page, top) was built in London its studios were placed at the heart of the building so that the surrounding offices and other accommodation would buffer the noise from the London streets outside.

Experimental rooms that require total silence need to deal with transmitted sound and reflected sound. To exclude reflected sound they are provided with absorbent surfaces. To prevent transmitted sound they have to have sealed doorways, and be detached from as much of the surrounding fabric of the building as possible.

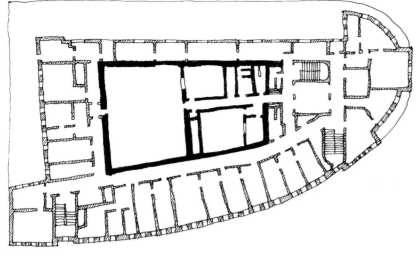

In his design for a performance platform in Crystal Palace Ian Ritchie provided a half-roof/half-wall which would help to reflect sound towards the audience.

Reference for Ian Ritchie's stage at Crystal Palace:
RIBA Journal, April 1997, pp.28-9.

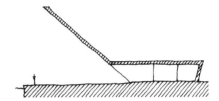

The studios of Broadcasting House were embedded in the heart of the building to help insulate them from outside noise.

The surfaces of the internal walls of the Royal Festival Hall in London are balanced between absorption and reflection to optimise the sound the audience hears from the performers. The ceiling, however, was found to be too low to give the optimal reverberation needed for music, so loudspeakers were introduced into the ceiling to increase the reverberation time artificially.

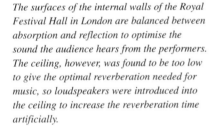

Different sorts of performance benefit from different arrangements of wall surfaces, so halls designed for the performance of music can be different in their shape and in the composition of their walls from theatres designed mainly for performance involving speech. Their 'reverberation times' – the time it takes for sound to die out – will be different. Speech benefits from a shorter reverberation time; music benefits from a slightly longer reverberation time. The ceilings and seating areas, as well as the walls, of such performance places contribute to the acoustic character of the spaces.

The concert hall in the Royal Festival Hall (below) is buffered from outside sounds by the surrounding foyers and offices. Inside, its surfaces were balanced between reflectivity and absorption to optimise the way the ears of the audience receive the sound from the performers. Even so, once it was built and used, it was found that the ceiling was too low to give the optimum reflections, so it was fitted with loudspeakers to lengthen the reverberation time artificially.

These are functions of walls, and affect decisions about how they are positioned, and the ways in which they are built. They affect the materials chosen and their surface finish. They condition the character and identity of the places walls help to make.

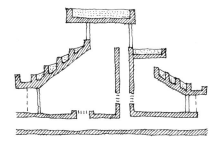

The Fusui-no-ie house (right; its name means 'house of the winds and waters'), designed by Team Zoo, and built in Japan in 1979, has double outer walls that protect its interior from the heat and humidity of the Okinawa summer. A wall at the centre of the house draws, by stack effect (the natural tendency of warm air to rise), ventilating and cooling breezes through ducts under the floor.

Reference for Fusui-no-ie house:
Manfred Spiedel (editor) – *Team Zoo: buildings and projects 1971-1990*, 1991, p.42.

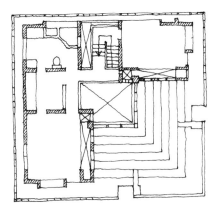

Heat

Since early times walls have been built to help people keep warm, by sheltering them from weather and cold. The ways in which walls modify temperature are various. Certainly they shelter space within from wind, but they can also absorb and store heat from the sun.

Walk into a simple garden shed, with walls painted black, on a sunny day. Even if the air temperature outside is cool, the inside of the shed will be warm from the heat absorbed by the matt black surfaces of the shed's walls. This is why caravans and mobile homes usually have their walls and roofs painted white, or (even better) polished to a silvered finish... to reflect away as much of the sun's heat as possible, and avoid the inside becoming overheated.

It may have been that the rows of columns surrounding the cella of a temple, together with the roof they supported, helped to keep the interior cooler than it would otherwise have been, by shading it from the hot Greek sun.

The same device is used in many hot countries... the verandahs of the traditional timber houses of Malaysia and Queensland, Australia, are examples. The walls of such houses are made as open as possible, and the floors raised from the ground on piles, to allow as much cross-ventilation as pos-

The column supported overhangs of the roofs of Greek temples may have helped keep the interior cool under the hot Greek sun.

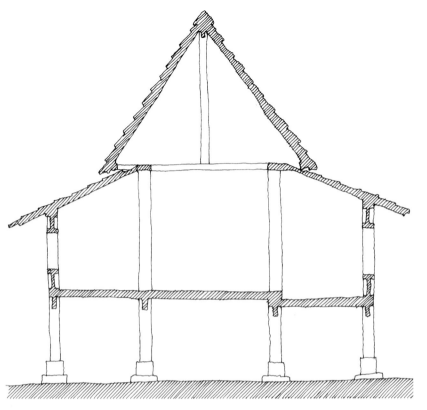

The same device is used in the houses of many hot countries. Above is the section through a typical Malay house in Malaysia. The walls are kept as open as possible, and the floor is raised from the ground, to allow cross-ventilation. The roof also overhangs to shade the walls and prevent them from heating the interior.

sible. But they also have roofs with deep overhangs to shade the walls and prevent them from becoming hot and warming the interior by radiation.

In some countries with hot climates walls are built with ventilation shafts within them. The example below is of an 'Oriental' house in Iraq. The walls to the street are cantilevered to increase the shade. The wall away from the street, to the right of the drawing, has four ventilation shafts built into the wall, with scoops at roof level to catch breezes and bring them into the house.

In countries with cooler climates the problem is more to keep warm than keep cool. The capacity of walls to absorb and store heat has been used in various ways.

In this house in Iraq the back wall is fitted with ventilation shafts, topped by scoops that catch passing breezes and bring them into the interior.

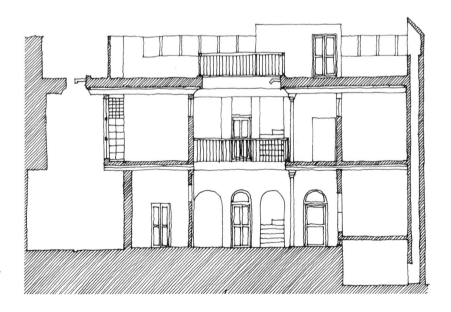

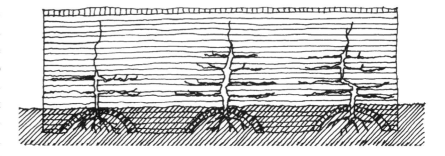

Gardeners have been using the heat-retentive properties of walls for hundreds of years. Many plants grow well on the protected sunny side of a wall, but they also benefit from the warmth the wall stores during a sunny day and releases slowly at night. The walls were an essential instrument of productivity in a Victorian kitchen garden. Often they were built of a soft reddy-orange clay brick, a colour that readily absorbs the warming rays from the sun, and is good at radiating that heat too. Fruit trees grown against them benefit from warmth stored in and given out by the bricks, particularly in early spring nights when frosts could damage fruit buds.

Some gardeners even built what were called 'hot' walls. The drawing below shows a section through a hot wall, illustrating the flues that were built into the wall to carry heat from a furnace through-out the wall's fabric, warming the air around plants grown along them.

And of course, since glass became more readily available in the nineteenth century, gardeners have used it for greenhouses. The back wall of a 'lean-to' greenhouse helps store the warmth collected during the day, and keeps the plants warm during the cooler nights.

Walls can also store heat introduced artificially into buildings. The fireplace wall or chimney stack, as well as carrying

Many types of plants benefit from being grown on the sunny side of a wall. The wall protects them from wind, but also can store warmth.

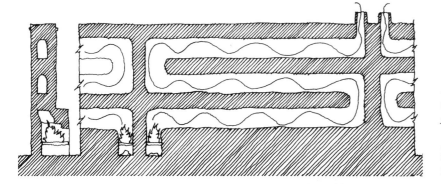

Some gardeners built 'hot' walls, incorporating flues which carried hot air from fires through the fabric.

Reference for 'hot' walls:
Susan Campbell – *Charleston Kedding*, 1996, p.42.

194

Walls containing chimney stacks store some of the heat from the fire. When they are positioned between rooms the warmth benefits both.

Reference for Pwll-pridd, Llanidloes Without, and Old Packhorse Inn, Welshpool:
Peter Smith – *Houses of the Welsh Country-side*, 1975.

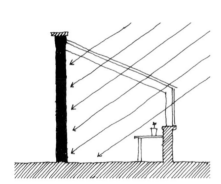

The back wall of a 'lean-to' greenhouse (above) helps store heat collected through the glass.

A 'Trombe' wall (right) stores heat gathered through glass to radiate it into the interior of a house.

Reference for the Trombe-Michel House, Odeillo:
Dean Hawkes – *The Environmental Tradition*, 1996.

away fumes from the fire through the flue, acts as a storage heater spreading the warmth of the fire through the house.

When fires were burnt in the centre of living spaces, without chimney stacks, there was nothing, apart from perhaps the floor or some large stone used as a fire

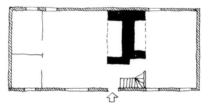

back, to store the fire's heat. But when fireplaces were built into the walls of houses then the walls themselves became stores of heat, radiating heat slowly to supplement the more direct radiant heat from the fire itself.

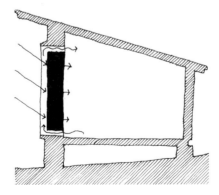

Sometimes fireplaces and chimney stacks were built on outside walls, but when the walls that accommodated them were built between two rooms then both would benefit from the stored heat. The apparent comfort of a space is affected as much by the surface temperature of its walls as it is

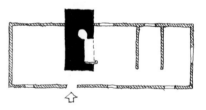

by the actual temperature of the air it contains. Allowing a fire to warm the fabric of the walls as well as the air increases the apparent comfort of the room substantially.

When the nineteenth-century architect Philip Webb designed Standen in Sussex (1891, overleaf), he built a conservatory onto the south-facing front of the house to provide a place for growing exotic plants such as Bougainvillea. The space helped warm other parts of the house too, by warming its surrounding walls, and by allowing warm air to drift into adjacent rooms.

When he was planning the house, Webb also made sure that all the chimney stacks were positioned within the mass of

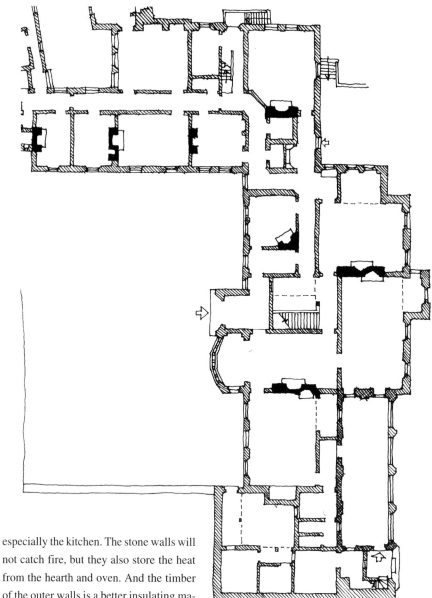

the house so that heat was not wasted to the outside air but warmed the living space within.

This small farmhouse in the Trentino district of Italy (below) uses something of the same principle. Although the outer fabric of the house is built mainly in timber, its core is built of stone. These stone rooms accommodate the places where there is fire,

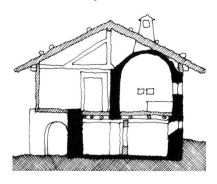

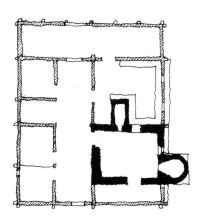

especially the kitchen. The stone walls will not catch fire, but they also store the heat from the hearth and oven. And the timber of the outer walls is a better insulating material than stone, and so helps to keep the warmth inside the house.

In times when the cost of energy required to heat the inside of buildings and expectations of comfort are high, it is necessary that walls are good at providing thermal insulation. The walls of most buildings built in Britain now have plenty of insula-

In this old Italian farmhouse (far left) there is a stone core of rooms within a timber outer structure. The stone rooms are those where there are sources of warmth, and the masonry helps to store the heat, releasing it slowly into the rest of the house.

196

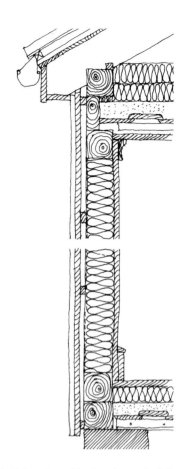

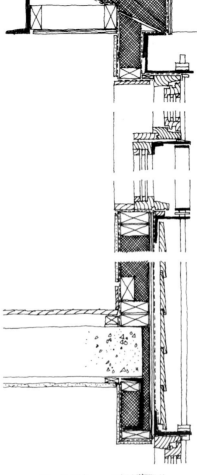

Philip Webb designed Standen in Sussex (left) so that the walls containing the chimney stacks were always between two rooms, so that warmth from the fires would not be wasted to the outside air.

Reference for Standen:
W.R. Lethaby – *Philip Webb and his Work*, 1979.

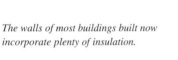

The walls of most buildings built now incorporate plenty of insulation.

Reference for Richard Murphy's housing: Architect's Journal, 18/23 December 1999, p.40.

Reference for Norwegian timber houses: Drange, Aanensen and Brænne – *Gamle Trehus*, (Oslo) 1980.

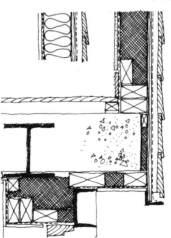

tion built into them. The drawing to the left is a cross section through one of the walls of Richard Murphy's housing at the Canongate in Edinburgh, and built in 1999. The insulation is shown cross-hatched to emphasise it. (Usually, in such a drawing, the convention for showing insulation is a wavy line, as shown in the small inset.) The dotted lines shown are 'vapour checks', which prevent moist air from dampening the insulation and reducing its effectiveness.

In climates with even harsher winters, even more insulation is beneficial. The above drawing shows the insulation in a refurbished traditional timber house in Norway.

197

And when Ralph Erskine built a simple house for himself in Sweden in the 1940s he designed the north wall to incorporate wood storage and bookcases. The logs and books contributed to the insulation of the wall.

Notice too that Erskine placed the hearth and its chimney stack wall centrally, between the kitchen and the living space, so that it would store heat and warm the inside rather than outside space. He inserted open-ended clay pipes horizontally into the stack to allow the air to pick up more of the warmth from the stone wall heated by the fire. The south wall is largely glazed so that it benefits from passive solar gains from the low-angle sun in the winter; though it is shaded by the overhang of the roof against excessive high-angle sun in the summer.

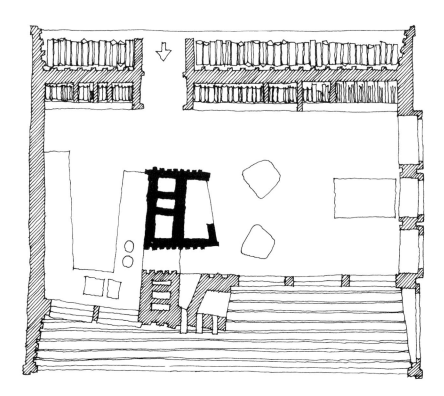

Reference for Ralph Erskine's own house: Peter Collymore – *The Architecture of Ralph Erskine*, 1985.

Light

"The elements of architecture are light and shade, walls and space."

Le Corbusier, translated by Frederick Etchells – *Towards a New Architecture*, 1923 (1927), p.177.

Solid opaque walls cannot usually store or transmit light. But light is one of the most important elements modified by walls. Walls can insulate a place against light – as in a photographic darkroom, or a cinema – but they also provide surfaces on which light falls, and off which it may be reflected. Walls are screens for light. Without light they cannot be seen.

You can draw or write in light on a wall, by scratching or chiselling into the surface. The marks make light and dark surfaces, which can be read, sculpturally or verbally.

You can exaggerate the expression of construction by making joints that create shadows.

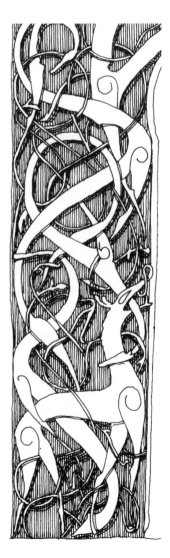

Vikings decorated the timber walls of their stave churches with elaborate low-relief carvings of stylised mythical animals, obscuring the material of the walls with intricate patterns of light and shade.

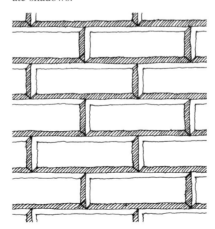

Expression of the construction of a wall can be exaggerated by deepening the joints, making shadows.

When he wanted to record his Modulor system for proportions and dimensions on a buildings, Le Corbusier had it cast into the poured concrete walls (below). The images and measurements are read, not by line, but by light and shade.

Much of architectural ornamentation, of whatever historical style, has been concerned with light and shade. Though drawn in line, their effect is seen in light. In the classical language of architecture, for example, there is an extensive repertoire of details designed to catch light and cast shadows. Students of architecture when Classicism was the dominant mode of design spent much time learning skiagraphy – the projection of shadows in drawing.

Most of the 'architecture' of this niche on St Peter's in Rome is concerned with 'drawing' with light on the wall of the church. This niche was illustrated in a photograph in Le Corbusier's book Towards a New Architecture *(translated by Frederick Etchells in 1927).*

Reference for Le Corbusier's Modulor:
Le Corbusier, translated by de Francia and Bostock – *The Modulor: a harmonious measure to the human scale universally applicable to architecture and mechanics,* 1961.

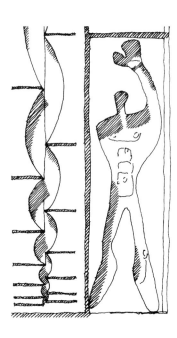

"*Our elements are vertical walls, the spread of the soil, holes to serve as passages for man or for light, doors or windows. The holes give much or little light, make gay or sad. The walls are in full brilliant light, or in half shade or in full shade, giving an effect of gaiety, serenity or sadness. Your symphony is made ready. The aim of architecture is to make you gay or serene. Have respect for walls. The Pompeian did not cut up his wall-spaces; he was devoted to wall-spaces and loved light. Light is intense when it falls between walls which reflect it. The ancients built walls, walls which stretch out and meet to amplify the wall. In this way they created volumes, which are the basis of architectural and sensorial feeling. The light bursts on you, by a definite intention, at one end and illuminates the walls. The* impression *of light is extended outside by cylinders (I hardly like to say columns, it is a worn-out word), peristyles or pillars.*

Le Corbusier, translated by Frederick Etchells – *Towards a New Architecture*, 1923 (1927), pp.185-6.

In the thick south wall of his pilgrimage chapel at Ronchamp (below and right), Le Corbusier cut deep windows with splayed jambs, cills and heads. They open the inaccessible matter of the wall, and wash the 'cut' surfaces with sunlight coloured by glass.

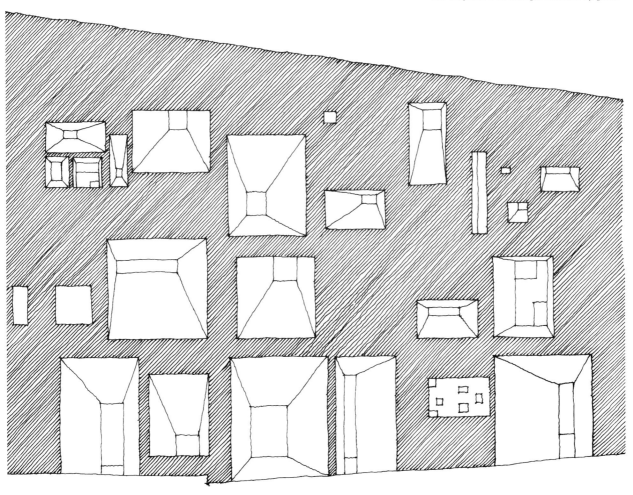

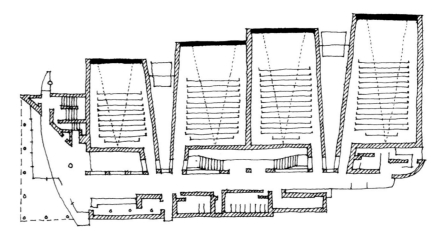

Reference for the chapel at Ronchamp:
W. Boesiger – *Le Corbusier: œuvre complète
(Volume 5) 1946-1952*, 1995, pp.72-84.

*James Turrell has worked with light and
space. But many of his projects depend on
walls. The wall, though inanimate, is the
catalyst for the effect he wants to achieve. In
Pleiades (below) he projected very low levels
of light onto a wall. He described the effect:*

*"Pleiades is a Dark Piece where the realm of
night vision touches the realm of eyes-closed
vision, where the space generated is
substantially different than the physical
confines and is not dependent upon it, where
the seeing that comes from 'out there' merges
with the seeing that comes from 'in here,'
where the seeing develops over and through
dark adaptation but continues beyond it."*

*Cinemas 'work' by the projection of images in
light onto a screen wall. The wall disappears,
behind the illusion of moving images. But
without the wall the images would be lost,
dispersed into infinite space.*

Reference for Pleiades *(1989) by James
Turrell:*
http://www.mattress.lm.com/Catalogue/turrell.html

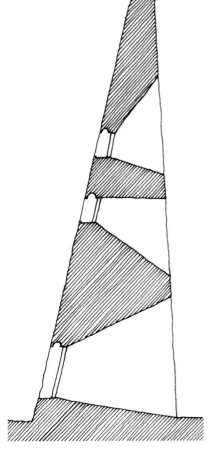

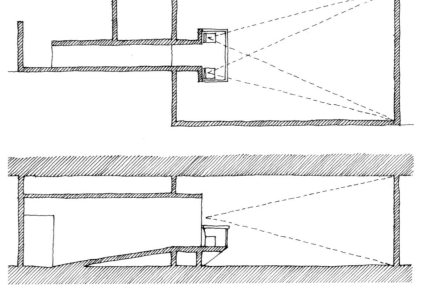

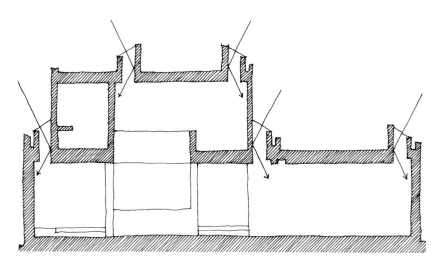

Leslie Martin's refurbishment and extension of Kettle's Yard in Cambridge (1970, above) involved provision of gallery spaces which could also be used for living. The walls are washed with a soft reflected light, through raised roof lights along the edges of the spaces, ideal for lighting the sculpture and paintings displayed.

Reference for Kettle's Yard, Cambridge, U.K.: Dean Hawkes – *The Environmental Tradition: studies in the architecture of environment,* 1996, p.110.

In the Breakfast Room of his own house in Lincoln's Inn Fields, London (below), John Soane developed a subtle way of modifying the light from the sky that fell on the pictures hung on its walls. The walls reflected a hidden light from the sky into the room.

Reference for John Soane's own house: John Summerson – 'The Soane Museum, 13 Lincoln's Inn Fields', in *Architectural Monographs: John Soane*, 1983, pp.25-39.

"'Look,' he said, pointing at the clean, white wall on the other side of the room. Dark bookshelves flanked the wall, and a black girder bisected it. 'Look at that wall carefully and you'll of course see that its whiteness is not of just one tone. The light is streaming in from the window, so that it's a brighter white to that side, fading into grays over to this side. There are blues and greens and even purples. It's a little bit more difficult to see the incidental transitions, the low-grade shadows caused by the varying textures, because of the starkness of contrast between the white wall and the black plank. Still, if I were to daub a slash of red paint in that corner, it would change the whiteness of the entire field....'"

Robert Irwin quoted in Lawrence Weschler – *Seeing is Forgetting the Name of the Thing One Sees: a life of contemporary artist Robert Irwin*, 1982, pp.71-2.

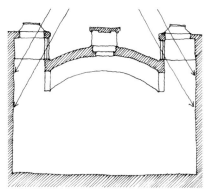

In his Crystallographic Data Centre in Cambridge (1992, right), Eric Sørensen used walls for keeping direct sunlight out of spaces where computers would be used, and also for reflecting a softer, more diffused light into those spaces. The reflecting wall also became a screen on which the moving patterns of the sun and its shadows was projected.

Reference for the Crystallographic Data Centre, Cambridge, U.K.:
Dean Hawkes – *The Environmental Tradition: studies in the architecture of environment*, 1996, 182-9.

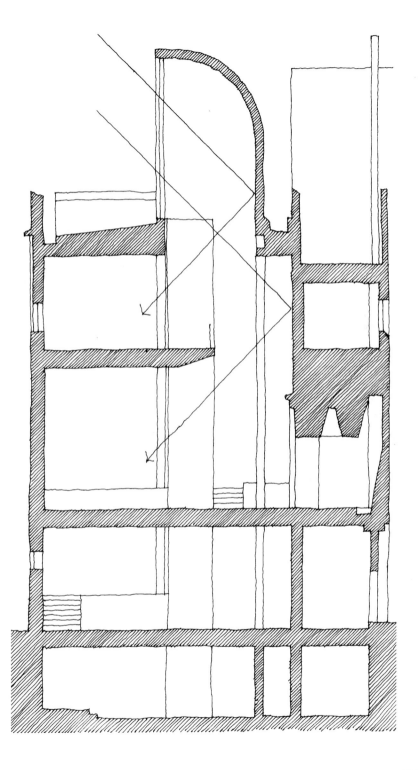

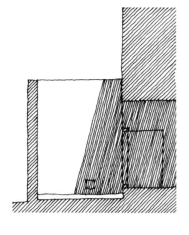
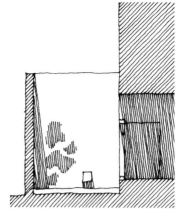

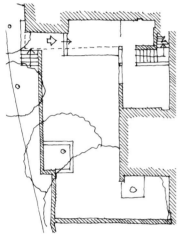
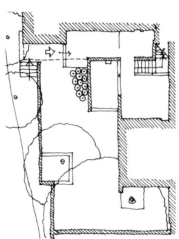

Reference for the Antonio Gálvez House:
Raúl Rispa (editor) – *Barragán: the complete works*, 1996, pp.138-45.

In his design for the Antonio Gálvez House in Mexico City (1955), Luis Barragán included an extra external wall near the entrance. The pink L-shaped wall contains a shallow pool of water fed by a gentle fountain fixed to the shorter length. The wall does a number of things. It screens one of the main rooms of the house from the sight of someone entering the gateway into the front yard. It also modifies and lengthens the transition zone entering the front door. But perhaps most powerfully it acts as a screen on which the moving shadows of the sun are projected, creating a dynamic work of art appreciable from inside the house, and reflecting sunlight into its dark interior. The three drawings above show three stages in an infinite sequence of patterns of light and shade projected onto the wall and reflected into the house.

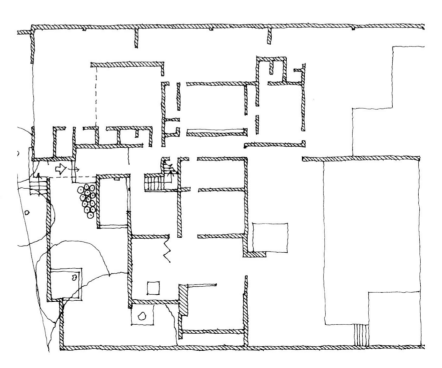

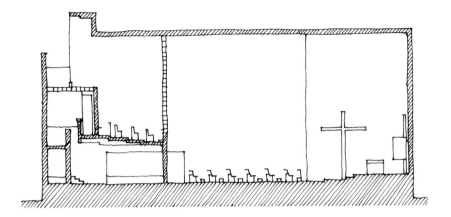

Barragán was a great exponent of the wall in architecture, and was especially sensitive to its potential as a receptor and reflector of light, often coloured by applied pigment. The use of deeply coloured walls is a tradition under the strong sunlight of Mexico, and Barragán carried it to poetic levels.

In his Chapel for the Capuchinas (1952-55), also in Mexico City, he used coloured walls in many different ways: as screens, as backdrops, as reflectors.... The main cross in the chapel stands to one side in its own space. The space, and especially the terracotta-coloured wall behind the cross, is lit by a diffused yellowish light entering through a tall, narrow window hidden from the pews.

[The image used as the title page for the Preface to this Notebook is from Barragán's José Clemente Orozco House in Guadalajara (1934).]

Reference for the Chapel for the Capuchinas: Raúl Rispa (editor) – Barragán: the complete works, 1996, pp.146-59.

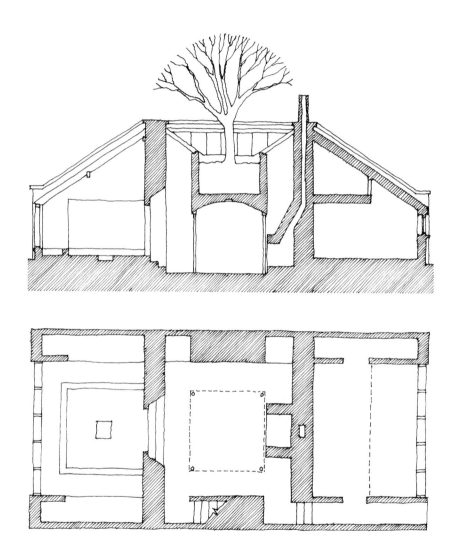

POSTSCRIPT

POSTSCRIPT

"This is the process of intellectual appropriation whereby we attempt in countless ways to form our vast number of impressions into a mental construct and to make them our own intellectual property. For even if the complete content of the human mind is to be considered dependent upon whatever comes into it from without, nothing can be our intellectual property that has not previously been a product of our thought. This process of appropriation finds its highest expression in the acquisition of scientific knowledge and in artistic creation, for both give rise to mental constructs in which we take possession of something that is in the world. We may readily admit that such an intellectual appropriation underlies the creation of works of painting, sculpture, and even poetry, but in architecture it seems almost impossible to prove the existence of a comparable intellectual endeavour. And yet the tendency to subordinate to the form of the building the expression of those material requirements on which the existence of the building depends indicates that here, too, we start from certain given premises and rise by gradual process of formal creation to a result that is truly a thing of the mind. Only when the building has become a pure expression of form is the intellectual work of creation of form complete; and only then does it become, in the highest sense, a product and possession of the human mind – and only then, as a work of art, is it among the noblest manifestations of the human spirit. We must therefore proceed on the assumption that in architecture, as in every intellectual activity, there is a progression from the unformed to the formed. If we inquire as to the general nature of the elementary material to be formed, we find that it is none other than the basis of the initial practical need: enclosed, covered space."

Conrad Fiedler, translated by Mallgrave and Ikonomou – 'Observations on the Nature and History of Architecture' (1878), in Mallgrave and Ikonomou (editors) – *Empathy, Form and Space*, 1994, p.125.

Walls may be beautiful, or not... intellectually, metaphorically, aesthetically. Works of architecture are manifestations of a mind ordering the world according to its needs and desires. What I appreciate in 'good' architecture, as in a 'good' film, a 'good' play, a 'good' piece of music..., is empathy with the mind (like mine) that made it, gave it form. I flatter myself; I think, "I could do that!" In analysing a work of architecture I am fascinated to see another mind at work, responding to conditions, imposing order, playing with metaphors, evoking emotional responses... having ideas, refining and implementing them.

Architecture is a 'bridge' between minds. At one level architects organise places for others to use; they are 'gods' who set the frames of people's lives. At another level, they indulge in communication with each other through their work, challenging competitors, impressing critics, and paying homage to those who have influenced them as they go. Both levels constitute the vitality of architecture.

As I come to the end of putting this *Notebook* together I am most conscious of all the things that have been left out, or which could have been explored in more depth and detail. The subject appeared fairly simple as I set out, but time and again complexities and subtleties emerged. The wall is a rich invention, with many powers... more than I realised.

But no architect wants to know all the things that are in a *Notebook* like this; at least, not all at once. Taken together this is knowledge that can paralyse a designer's mind. With so many possibilities of how to make a wall, and of what a wall can do, how on earth (literally) can one make a decision?

Design is no matter of condensation to a right answer. It is divergent, before it is convergent. Excitement lies in infinite possibility... in following paths to who-knows-where. But there are pointers to unexplored territory....

The scope of architecture in the future is not limited by its history, but invention generally depends on an awareness of what has been done in the past. All architects exploit ideas that have been conceived, discovered, developed by others before them. By experiment they test their applicability in new situations. By creative imagination, they metamorphose them into subtle hybrids. By evoking their contraries, they try to provoke novelties. And so on. Ideas from the past hold no unquestionable authority over the present, but they can help an architect find a path....

A Note on Methodology

Some writers on architecture have recognised apparent shortcomings in ways in which their subject is sometimes described and categorised.

Over a hundred years ago, August Schmarsow suggested that the way in which architecture was understood should be overhauled, in the interest of re-establishing an (apparently lost) vital relation with people and life.

"Indeed, today it seems as if nobody knows what constitutes architecture. Notwithstanding all our historical erudition, we have everywhere a vague feeling of alienation; we feel no inner, human warmth in its works; it is an art to which we lack a natural relation.... Is it not time to inquire into the origin and innermost essence of architecture?"(1)

Some twenty years later, on a related theme, William Richard Lethaby implicitly criticised the role of architectural historians in building a classification system for architecture which, rather than clarifying its fundamental powers and making them accessible for use, obscured them under categories associated primarily with superficial appearances – 'styles'.

"Modern builders need a classification of architectural factors irrespective of time and country, a classification by essential variation.... In architecture more than anywhere we are the slaves of names and categories, and so long as the whole field of past architectural experiment is presented to us accidentally only under historical schedules, designing architecture is likely to be conceived as scholarship rather than as the adaptation of its accumulated powers to immediate needs..."(2)

Sixty years after that, Alberto Perez-Gomez condemned the appropriation of the word 'theory' by science to refer to 'a methodology which if put into practice would produce specific results', and the application of that definition to architecture. By implication he suggested 'theory' might alternatively be better seen as a matter of 'making sense', and that what was needed was not a methodology for doing architecture but a 'theory' which offered an understanding of how it works (similar perhaps to the ways in which grammar and music theory do not offer prescriptive methodologies for use of language or for musical composition respectively, but describe how they work).

(1) August Schmarsow, translated by Mallgrave and Ikonomou – 'The Essence of Architectural Creation' (1893), in Mallgrave and Ikonomou (editors) – *Empathy, Form and Space*, 1994.

(2) W.R. Lethaby – *Architecture*, 1912, pp.8-9.

(3) Alberto Perez-Gomez – *Architecture and the Crisis of Modern Science*, 1983, p.5.

(4) Robin Evans – *The Projective Cast: architecture and its three geometries*, 1995, p.xxxvi.

(5) Peter Jones – '(Why right words matter...) ... and how they work in practice', in *The Daily Telegraph*, 18 June 1996.

"Today, theory in any discipline is generally identified with methodology; it has become a specialized set of prescriptive rules concerned with technological values, that is, with process rather than ultimate objectives, a process that seeks maximum efficiency with minimum effort."(3)

And in the 1990s, Robin Evans echoed Schmarsow, Lethaby, and Perez-Gomez by suggesting that architecture should be 'grown-up' enough to have its own (not methodologically prescriptive) theory, rather than ones derived by analogy from language or mathematics (or for that matter, one might infer, art history or music).

"A lot can be learned from literary theory, not least circumspection, also a sufficient confidence that the subject for which a theory is being sought is itself worthy of some modest consultation in the matter. In architecture the trouble has been that a superior paradigm derived either from mathematics, the natural sciences, the human sciences, painting, or literature has always been ready at hand. They have supplied us with our needs at some cost. We beg our theories from these more highly developed regions only to find architecture annexed to them as a satellite subject. Why is it not possible to derive a theory of architecture from a consideration of architecture?"(4)

In their limited way, this *Notebook* and its predecessor are products of attempts to respond to concerns similar to those expressed by these writers, and to try to help build a 'theory' of architecture derived from observation and analysis of examples.

They try to do this in a way similar to that by which the study of language is described by Peter Jones in the following passage:

"... grammar is the study of the different forms of language. It examines texts, observes what is common to them, and deduces appropriate categories of definition and description from them. It describes linguistic usage in terms of the origins and meanings words have (etymology and semantics), the forms words take (inflexion, also including the sounds of words, phonetics) and how words are put together to form meaningful utterances (syntax). In other words, it is a descriptive exercise, not a prescriptive one."(5)

BIBLIOGRAPHY

Friedrich Achleitner (introduction) – *Walter Pichler: drawings, sculpture, buildings*, Princeton Architectural Press, Princeton, 1994.

Peter Aldington – *Three Houses and a Garden*, Garden Art, Woodbridge, 1998.

William Alex – *Japanese Architecture*, Prentice-Hall, London, 1965.

A. Balfour – *Berlin: the politics of order, 1737-1989*, Rizzoli, New York, 1990.

A. Becker, J. Olley and W. Wang (editors) – *Twentieth Century Architecture, Ireland*, Prestel, Munich and New York, 1997.

Peter Blake (editor) – *Marcel Breuer: Sun and Shadow, the philosophy of an architect*, Longmans, London, undated.

Reginald Blomfield – 'The Architect of Newgate', in *Studies in Architecture*, Macmillan & Co., London, 1905.

W. Boesiger (editor) – *Le Corbusier: œuvre complète*, Max Bill, Zurich, 1995.

Frank E. Brown – *Roman Architecture*, Prentice-Hall, London, 1964.

Jan Butterfield (editor) – *The Art of Light and Space*, Abbeville, New York, 1993.

Italo Calvino, translated by William Weaver – *Invisible Cities*, Harcourt Brace & Co., San Diego, New York, London, 1972.

Susan Campbell – *Charleston Kedding: a history of kitchen gardening*, Ebury Press, London, 1996.

Rhys Carpenter – *The Architects of the Parthenon*, Penguin, Harmondsworth, 1970.

Francisco Asensio Cerver – *International Landscape Architecture*, Barcelona, 1997.

Giorgio Ciucci – *Giuseppe Terragni : opera completa*, Electa, Milan, 1996.

Peter Collymore – *The Architecture of Ralph Erskine*, Architext, London, 1994.

Caroline Constant – *The Woodland Chapel: towards a spiritual landscape*, Byggforlaget, Stockholm, 1994.

Jackie Cooper – *Mackintosh, Architecture*, Academy Editions, London, 1977.

Glyn E. Daniel – *The Prehistoric Chamber Tombs of England and Wales*, Cambridge University Press, Cambridge, 1950.

John Donat (editor) – *World Architecture 1*, Studio Vista, London, 1964.

John Donat (editor) – *World Architecture 2*, Studio Vista, London, 1965.

Drange, Aanensen and Brænne – *Gamle Trehus*, Universitetsforlaget, Oslo, 1980.

Claes Dymling and others – *Architect, Sigurd Lewerentz*, Byggforlaget, Stockholm, 1997.

Umberto Eco, translated by William Weaver – *The Name of the Rose*, Minerva, London, 1983.

I.E.S. Edwards – *The Pyramids of Egypt*, Penguin, Harmondsworth, 1971.

Mircea Eliade, translated by Rosemary Sheed – *Patterns in Comparative Religion*, University of Nebraska Press, London, 1958.

Mircea Eliade, translated by Willard R. Trask – *The Sacred and the Profane: the nature of religion*, Harvest Books, New York, 1959.

Robin Evans – *The Projective Cast: architecture and its three geometries*, MIT Press, Cambridge Mass., 1995.

Herman Fabini – *Atlas der siebenbürgisch-sächsischen Kirchenburgen und Dorfkirchen*, Sibiu, 1999.

Conrad Fiedler, tramslated by Harry Francis Mallgrave and Eleftherios Ikonomou – 'Observations on the Nature and History of Architecture' (1878), in Malgrave and Ikonomou (editors) – *Empathy, Form and Space*, The Getty Center for the History of Art and Architecture, Santa Monica, 1994.

Miljenko Foretic – *Dubrovnik*, Grafoprint, Dubrovnik, 1997.

Kenneth Frampton and Charles Correa – *Charles Correa*, Thames & Hudson, London, 1996.

Masao Furuyama – *Tadao Ando*, Artemis, London, 1993.

Andy Goldsworthy – *Wood*, Viking, London, 1996.

John Graby (editor) – *150 Years of Architecture in Ireland, The Royal Institute of the Architects of Ireland 1839-1989*, RIAI with Eblana Editions, Dublin, 1989.

James Walter Graham – *The Palaces of Crete*, Princeton University Press, Princeton, 1962.

Robert Graves – *The Greek Myths* (two volumes), Penguin, Harmondsworth, 1955.

Diane Haigh – *Baillie Scott, the artistic house*, Academy Editions, London, 1995.

John F. Harbeson – *The Study of Architectural Design*, Pencil Points Press, New York, 1927.

Richard Haslam – *Clough Williams-Ellis*, Academy Editions, London, 1996.

Dean Hawkes – *The Environmental Tradition*, E&F.N. Spon, London, 1996.

Seamus Heaney – 'From Maecenas to MacAlpine', in John Graby (editor) – *150 Years of Architecture in Ireland, The Royal Institute of the Architects of Ireland 1839-1989*, RIAI with Eblana Editions, Dublin, 1989.

Martin Heidegger, translated by Albert Hofstadter – 'Building Dwelling Thinking' (1952), in *Poetry, Language, Thought*, Harper & Row, New York, 1975.

Wolfgang Hermann – *Gottfried Semper: in search of architecture*, MIT Press, Cambridge Mass., 1989

Hermann Hesse, translated by Basil Creighton – *Steppenwolf* (1927), Penguin, Harmondsworth, 1980.

Roger Hinks, edited by John Goldsmith – *The Gymnasium of the Mind*, Michael Russell, Salisbury, 1984.

John D. Hoag – *Western Islamic Architecture*, Prentice-Hall, London, 1964.

Robert Hooper – *Laurent Pariente*, Henry Moore Sculpture Trust, Leeds, 1996.

John James – *The Contractors of Chartres* (two volumes), Mandorla, Wyong, Australia, 1981.

Eugene J. Johnson – *Drawn from the Source: the travel sketches of Louis I. Kahn*, MIT Press, Cambridge, Mass., 1996.

Philip Johnson – *Mies van der Rohe*, Secker & Warburg, London, 1978.

Peter Jones – '(Why right words matter...) ... and how they work in practice', in *The Daily Telegraph*, 18 June 1996.

James Joyce – *Ulysses* (1922), Penguin, Harmondsworth, 1992.

G.E. Kidder-Smith – *Italy Builds*, Architectural Press, London, 1954.

Hisao Koyama – *Louis I. Kahn, Conception and Meaning*, A&U, Tokyo, 1983.

John Krause – *Two Churches*, Arkitectur Forlag, Stockholm, 1997.

D. F. Krell – *Archeticture* (sic)*: Ecstasies of Space, Time and the Human Body*, State University of New York Press, New York, 1997.

A.W. Lawrence – *Greek Architecture*, Penguin, Harmondsworth, 1957.

Le Corbusier, edited, annotated, and translated by Ivan Zaknic in collaboration with Nicole Pertuiset – *Journey to the East*, MIT Press, Cambridge, Mass., 1987.

Le Corbusier, translated by de Francia and Bostock – *The Modulor: a harmonious measure to the human scale universally applicable to architecture and mechanics*, Faber & Faber, London, 1961.

Le Corbusier, translated by Frederick Etchells – *Towards a New Architecture* (1923), John Rodker, London, 1927.

W.R. Lethaby – *Architecture: an introduction to the history and theory of the art of building*, Williams & Norgate, London, 1912.

W.R. Lethaby – *Architecture, Mysticism and Myth* (1892), Architectural Press, London, 1974.

W.R. Lethaby – *Philip Webb and his Work*, Raven Oak Press, London, 1979.

Harry Francis Mallgrave and Eleftherios Ikonomou (editors) – *Empathy, Form and Space*, The Getty Center for the History of Art and Architecture, Santa Monica, 1994.

Lionel March and Judith Scheine – *R.M. Schindler: Composition and Construction*, Academy Editions, London, 1993.

R.D. Martienssen – *The Idea of Space in Greek Architecture*, Witwatersrand University Press, Johannesburg, 1968.

Roland Martin – *Living Architecture: Greek*, Oldbourne, London, 1967.

David McLees – *Castell Coch*, Cadw: Welsh Historic Monuments, Cardiff, 1999.

Jeremy Melvin – 'Superfour', in the *Royal Institute of British Architects Journal*, September 1997.

David Mohney and Keller Easterling (editors) – *Seaside: making a town in America*, Phaidon, London, 1991.

Salomon Moshé – *Urban Anatomy in Jerusalem*, Technion, Haifa, 1996.

J.R. Mulryne and Margaret Shewring (editors) – *Shakespeare's Globe Rebuilt*, Cambridge University Press, Cambridge, 1997.

Richard Murphy – *Carlo Scarpa and Castelvecchio*, Butterworth, London, 1990.

Friedrich Nietzsche, translated by Francis Golffing – *The Birth of Tragedy*, 1871 (1956).

Christian Norberg-Schulz and Gennara Postiglione – *Sverre Fehn: Works, Projects, Writings, 1949-1996*, Monacelli Press, New York, 1997.

Michael Parker Pearson and Colin Richards – 'Architecture and Order: Spatial Representation and Archaeology', in *Architecture and Order*, Routledge, London, 1994.

J.D.S. Pendlebury – *A Handbook to the Palace of Minos at Knossos*, Macmillan, London, 1935.

Nigel Pennick – *Mazes and Labyrinths*, Turnstone Press, Wellingborough, 1990.

Walker Percy – *The Moviegoer*, quoted in Lawrence Weschler – *Seeing is Forgetting the Name of the Thing One Sees: a life of contemporary artist Robert Irwin*, 1982.

Georges Perec, translated by John Sturrock – *Species of Spaces and Other Pieces*, Penguin, Harmondsworth, 1974.

Alberto Perez-Gomez – *Architecture and the Crisis of Modern Science*, MIT Press, Cambridge, Mass., 1983.

Nikolaus Pevsner – *An Outline of European Architecture*, Penguin, Harmondsworth, 1945.

Plato, translated by Desmond Lee – *The Republic*, Penguin, Harmondsworth, 1955.

Marcel Proust, translated by C.K. Scott Moncrieff and Terence Kilmartin – *Swann's Way* (1913), Penguin, Harmondsworth, 1983.

A.W.N. Pugin – *Details of Ancient Timber Houses of the 15th & 16th centuries...*, Ackermann & Co., London, 1836.

Rainer Maria Rilke, translated by M.D. Herter Norton – *The Notebooks of Malte Laurids Brigge* (1910), W.W. Norton, New York, 1985.

Raúl Rispa (editor) – *Barragán, the complete works*, Thames & Hudson, London, 1996.

D.S. Robertson – *Greek and Roman Architecture*, Cambridge University Press, Cambridge, 1969.

Joseph Rykwert (Introduction) – *Richard Meier Architect 1964/84*, Rizzoli, New York, 1984.

Joseph and Anne Rykwert – *The Brothers Adam: the men and the style*, Collins, London, 1985.

Göran Schildt – *Sketches: Alvar Aalto*, MIT Press, Cambridge, Mass., 1978.

Rudolf Schindler, translated by Harry Francis Mallgrave – 'Modern Architecture: a Program' (1913), in Lionel March and Judith Scheine – *R.M. Schindler: composition and construction*, Academy Editions, London, 1993.

August Schmarsow, translated by Harry Francis Mallgrave and Eleftherios Ikonomou – 'The Essence of Architectural Creation' (1893), in Mallgrave and Ikonomou (editors) – *Empathy, Form and Space*, The Getty Center for the History of Art and Architecture, Santa Monica, 1994.

Carl Schuchhardt – *Schliemann's Discoveries of the Ancient World*, Avenel, New York, 1979.

Gottfried Semper, translated by Wolfgang Hermann – Introduction to 'Comparative Building Theory' (1850), in Wolfgang Hermann – *Gottfried Semper: in search of architecture*, MIT Press, Cambridge Mass., 1989.

J.C. Shepherd and G.A. Jellicoe – *Italian Gardens of the Renaissance* (1925), Academy Editions, London, 1986.

Peter Smith – *Houses of the Welsh Countryside*, Her Majesty's Stationery Office, London, 1975.

Oswald Spengler, translated by Charles Francis Atkinson – *The Decline of the West*, Volume 1, George Allen & Unwin, London, 1918.

Manfred Spiedel (editor) – *Team Zoo: buildings and projects 1971-1990*, Thames & Hudson, London, 1991.

James Steele – *Eames House*, Phaidon, London, 1994.

Deyan Sudjic – *Home: The Twentieth-Century House*, Laurence King, London, 1999.

John Summerson – 'The Soane Museum, 13 Lincoln's Inn Fields', in *Architectural Monographs: John Soane*, Academy Editions, London, 1983.

John Summerson – *Inigo Jones*, Penguin, London, 1966.

Christopher Tadgell – *The History of Architecture in India*, Phaidon, London, 1990.

Arnold Taylor – *Conwy Castle and Town Walls*, Cadw: Welsh Historic Monuments, Cardiff, 1998.

William Taylor – *Greek Architecture*, Arthur Barker, London, 1971.

Egon Tempel – *Finnish Architecture Today*, Otava, Helsinki, 1968.

Henry David Thoreau, edited by Joseph Wood Krutch – *Walden and Other Writings*, Bantam Books, Toronto, New York, London, 1854.

Simon Unwin – *Analysing Architecture*, Routledge, London and New York, 1997.

Dom H. van der Laan, translated by Richard Padovan – *Architectonic Space: fifteen lessons on the disposition of the human habitat*, E.J. Brill, Leiden, 1983.

Eugene Viollet-le-Duc, translated by Benjamin Bucknall – *The Habitations of Man in All Ages* (1876), Arno Press, New York, 1977.

Eugene Viollet-le-Duc, translated by Benjamin Bucknall – *Lectures on Architecture* (1860), Sampson Low, Marston, Searle & Rivington, London, 1877.

Carsten-Peter Warncke – *De Stijl 1917-31*, Taschen, Cologne, 1991.

John Welsh – *Modern House*, Phaidon, London, 1995.

Lawrence Weschler – *Seeing is Forgetting the Name of the Thing One Sees: a life of contemporary artist Robert Irwin*, University of California Press, Berkeley, Los Angeles, London, 1982.

Richard Weston – *Alvar Aalto*, Phaidon, London, 1995.

Walt Whitman, edited by Francis Murphy – *The Complete Poems*, Penguin, Harmondsworth, 1975.

Elisabeth Whittle – *A Guide to Ancient and Historic Wales: Glamorgan and Gwent*, Her Majesty's Stationery Office, London, 1992.

Oliver Wick – *James Turrell: Irish Sky Garden*, 1992.

James Wines – *SITE*, Rizzoli, New York, 1989.

Nelson I. Wu – *Chinese and Indian Architecture*, Prentice-Hall, London, 1964.

Bruno Zevi – *The Modern Language of Architecture*, University of Washington Press, Seattle, 1978.

INDEX